COSMOLOGIA

Also by Stuart Harris:

Themes and Images: Singaporean and Malaysian Poetry in English (1989)
The Human Factor: a critical guide to the novel by Graham Greene (1990)

COSMOLOGIA

A Sequence of Epic Poems

in Three Parts

comprising

Part One: The Economy of Vegetation (1791)
Part Two: The Loves of the Plants (1789)
Part Three: The Temple of Nature (1803)

by

Erasmus Darwin (1731 - 1802)

Edited by Stuart Harris

For our grandsons, Peter, William, and Nicholas

First Published in 2002 by Stuart Harris
3 Pingle Head, 171 Millhouses Lane, Sheffield S7 2HD
E-mail: SHarris647@aol.com

Printed by RPM Reprographics (Ltd.), Chichester

ISBN 0 9542151 0 9

CONTENTS Page

ACKNOWLEDGMENTS

First, I wish to acknowledge the enormous help and encouragement extended to me throughout the preparation of this text by Dr Desmond King-Hele, FRS. Without the constant support of Desmond's unique knowledge of all things Darwinian, this edition would have been so much the poorer.
Secondly, I wish to thank my wife, Marie, for the countless conversations about the poems, which have played such a crucial part in the evolution of this text.
Thirdly, I must thank Dr Jacqueline Labbe who, during her time at the University of Sheffield, supervised my early Darwin studies and was the perfect mentor during the development of my ideas about the sequential structuring of these three poems.
Fourthly, I should like to thank Professor Sally Shuttleworth of the University of Sheffield for her continuing interest in this project from the early days of my research in her Department.
Fifthly, I must thank the Chairman, Dr G.C.Cook, and the Council of Management of the Erasmus Darwin Foundation for their sustained support of this project over the years.
Finally, I must thank John Sanders and Ivor Mitchell of the Darwin Walk Trust of Lichfield for first introducing me to Erasmus Darwin's Lichfield, and for inviting me to contribute to their Newsletter and to publicise this new edition there.

FOREWORD by Dr Desmond King-Hele, FRS

Ever since the Erasmus Darwin Centre at Lichfield opened in April 1999, visitors have been asking, "Is there a modern edition of Erasmus Darwin's poems?" Now I am delighted to be able to welcome just that, a book bringing together all three of his major poems, which run to more than 6,000 lines.

Stuart Harris has edited these poems with meticulous attention, and I have read his new text carefully, suggesting some further textual improvements. He has succeeded admirably in his aim of producing a readable modern text, with revised punctuation. (He has massacred most of the confusing 'dashes' with which Darwin spattered his poems.) In addition, distracting initial capitals have been cut down to size when necessary, and there are helpful footnotes and glossaries.

Darwin won great public acclaim when his poem *The Loves of the Plants* was published in 1789 as Part II of a longer poem called *The Botanic Garden*. Everyone eagerly awaited Part I, which eventually came out in 1792 (though dated 1791), and was entitled *The Economy of Vegetation*. For the next six years Darwin was regarded as the leading English poet of the day, as is proved by the praise of the *literati* - William Cowper, William Hayley, Horace Walpole, S.T.Coleridge and others - quoted in my recent biography *Erasmus Darwin: a Life of Unequalled Achievement* (1999). Darwin's last long poem, *The Temple of Nature*, appeared in 1803, after his death.

Stuart Harris has brought these three poems together under the title *Cosmologia*. His title is most appropriate because all three poems reflect the progressive world-view of the man who has been called "Mr Enlightenment himself" and "the leading *philosophe* of late 18th-century England". The basis of *The Temple of Nature* is Darwin's evolutionary view of life's development "from a single living filament", a microscopic speck in primeval seas, through fishes and amphibians to land animals and eventually humankind, as he calls us. This speculative scenario, going beyond anything published by his grandson Charles, was triumphantly validated by the results of the recent human genome project.

The original poems have long scientific notes in support of the verse. To have included these notes would have made this book five times larger, and much more expensive. And it is the verse that made Darwin famous. I hope you will enjoy it.

INTRODUCTION

Erasmus Darwin published his first two epic poems curiously out of sequence: *The Botanic Garden*, Part Two, 'The Loves of the Plants' in 1789, followed by Part One, 'The Economy of Vegetation' in 1791. The third poem, *The Temple of Nature*; or 'The Origin of Society' was published posthumously in 1803. This proved too late for Darwin's poetic collaborator and memorialist, Anna Seward, to include it in her detailed analysis of Darwin's poetry in her *Memoirs of the Life of Doctor Darwin* of 1804. These circumstances have partly prevented a reading of the three poems as a coherent sequence: twelve cantos in all, and of roughly equal length. My intention in giving the new, over-arching title of *Cosmologia* to the three poems is to promote the following fresh reading of them.

Cosmologia offers a progressive sequence: Part One describes and dramatises the material basis of the universe through the ancient model of the Four Elements: fire, earth, water and air. Each element is given one of the four cantos in which the origin and evolution of the universe is explored, including humanity's cultural involvement with the elemental drama. This elemental model dominated philosophical thought and poetic imagination for at least two millennia, and Darwin's version of it is an effective device for describing much of our experience of the cosmos in which we live. Part Two brings us historically into the early years of the eighteenth century, and to the pioneering work in plant classification (and taxonomy in general) of the Swedish naturalist, Carolus Linnaeus. His systematic work effected a revolution in our understanding not only of plant reproduction, but also of the wider relationships between classes, orders, genera, and species in the natural economy. Linnaeus's work of classification was an essential preliminary to the evolutionary insights that followed. Part Three, written ten years later, moves forward from the elemental and taxonomic models of Parts One and Two into an evolutionary scenario. Here the birth of the cosmos, the emergence of life, the arrival of sexual reproduction and its consequences for the development of human society including the problem of good and evil, are scientifically and imaginatively presented. At the same time, it is not only the intellectual framework of this third part that has been reshaped by Darwin: his language and imagery also become more philosophically rigorous. In his 'Advertisement', Darwin declares that he wishes to lead the imaginative reader "from the looser analogies which dress out the imagery of poetry, to the stricter ones , which form the ratiocination of philosophy", and this is what we find as we progress through the three parts of *Cosmologia*. Darwin's conception in this sequence is truly epic, moving us through the history of the universe and through humankind's developing understanding of it.

The title *Cosmologia* is, I believe, appropriate for two main reasons: first, it accurately signifies the cosmic scope of Darwin's epic, which reaches back to the birth of the universe and moves forward with the progress both of human society and of the human mind; secondly, the title is analogous to the titles of Darwin's two prose works:

Zoonomia; or, 'The Laws of Organic Life' (1794), and *Phytologia*; or, 'The Philosophy of Agriculture and Gardening' (1800). Darwin's poetry and prose are very closely related: the systematic investigations and experiments discussed factually in his scientific prose furnish the material for the ideas and images in his poetry. Indeed,Darwin makes his methodology clear in his 'Advertisement': "the general design is...to inlist Imagination under the banner of Science."

Given Darwin's lifelong involvement in medicine; his knowledge of botany and the pharmacology of the 'physick garden'; his inventor's interest in many of the new technologies that forged the Industrial Revolution; and his strong belief in the Enlightenment agenda for the improvement of the human condition, *Cosmologia* is a wonderful celebration of life. Twenty-first century readers will find much in Darwin that resonates sympathetically with our modern attitudes, especially Darwin's sense of the unity of all life on earth. The corollary that *Homo sapiens* is a creature of nature whose habitats and habits are similar to those of other species: that people are 'elementals', utilising and depending on fire, earth, water and air; that our health and survival on this planet depends on the cultivation and conservation of plants; and that our most sophisticated intellectual faculties are encouraged to grow in relationship with the material forms and processes of nature; all these fit well with current thinking about our place in the natural scheme of things.

What the modern reader might not find so congenial is the 'supernatural' machinery of the poetry, such as the nymphs of fire, gnomes, aquatic nymphs, and sylphs. They, like Shakespeare's Caliban and Ariel, represent aspects of the natural world, and enable Darwin to present elemental events and processes in the poetic terms suitable to the classic form of the epic. Homer, Milton, and Pope would understand how this mechanism works, just as, like Darwin, they understood the poetic value of the whole pantheon of classical gods and goddesses.

The other obstacle for the modern reader in approaching *Cosmologia* might be the metrical form of the rhyming couplet. Darwin worked hard to manage the heroic couplet in such a way that its whole meaning and expression were far more important than its simple rhyme-scheme. Anna Seward describes Darwin as, "Absorbed in the resolve of bringing the couplet-measure to a degree of sonorous perfection...", and I would recommend that *Cosmologia* be read aloud, even to oneself, in order to appreciate the special resonances of Darwin's language and phrasing.

It is, finally, important to recognise that the language and imagery of the first or of any single page, is not identical with the language and imagery that might be found elsewhere in the poem. Darwin's progression through the three parts from the poetic to the philosophical modes is one guarantee of this. The 'special case' of the first fifty-eight lines of the poem is, however, another issue altogether. Darwin adopted, and adapted, these lines from an 'exordium' or introductory verses written by Anna Seward in Darwin's actual botanic garden near Lichfield. He placed them at the head of his epic no doubt in recognition of the compliment they paid to him as the 'genius' of the garden. In addition, however, these lines are the clearest evidence of the collaborative tendencies of Darwin's way of working. This does not merely show itself in such intertextuality, but also in his requests to other friends, such as James Watt, to provide him with the technical information he needed for his poem. *Cosmologia* is a poem rich in references to an encyclopaedic range of scientific and cultural data gleaned from Darwin's scientific friends and from his reading. Anna Seward's 'presence' in the introduction is an important personal and cultural phenomenon: she is the first of the feminine 'voices' (another is the Goddess of Botany herself) that provides the gender-balance so important in Darwin's view of life. Thus it is, perhaps, appropriate that she should have the final word:

> "Nor let it once be thought that any error in Dr Darwin's poetic system; any occasional deviation from perfection in the plan, arrangement, or execution of this his complicated work, ought to prevent its being considered as one of the richest effusions of the poetic mind, that has shed lustre over Europe in the eighteenth century."

Note from the Editor

The footnotes accompanying the text are of four kinds:

1. Those taken from Darwin's own footnotes to specific lines of the poem, which are therefore without specific acknowledgment.
2. Those taken from other parts of the poem, or from other writings of Darwin, and which have specific acknowledgment thus: [ED].
3. Those taken from Dr Samuel Johnson's *Dictionary of the English Language*, acknowledged thus: [JD].
4. Those which are editorial footnotes, acknowledged thus: [ed.]

The italicisation follows the early editions.

APOLOGIA

Cosmologia is an epic poem which, like Darwin's own Indian fig-tree, sent its aerial roots underground into "cold oblivion" for two centuries, only to flourish now as its "renovated beauty blooms". It is, I believe, a poem especially suited to this twenty-first century in a variety of ways.

First, it recognises the disciplines and discourses of science and technology as appropriate for poetry: "inlisting Imagination under the banner of Science", as Darwin expresses it. His synthesis of the "two cultures" is a model of Wilsonian "consilience": that projected leaping together of the arts and the sciences. Anna Seward, Darwin's poetic collaborator, judged that "the Botanic Garden forms a new class of poetry" in its "adapting the past and recent discoveries in natural and scientific philosophy to the purposes of heroic verse".

Secondly, Darwin's vision of life is "ecological", predicated on the essential unity and interdependence of the whole natural world. He postulates that all life evolved from "the first speck of animated earth", and defines the moral imperatives implicit in his vision:

"Whence drew the enlightened Sage the moral plan,
That man should ever be the friend of man;
Should eye with tenderness all living forms,
His brother-emmets [ants] and his sister-worms."

Thirdly, Darwin confronts the intransigent problems of natural disasters and war; of fertility and food production; of diseases, mental disorders, and death in the natural world. His vision is uncompromising: "And one great slaughter-house the warring world." However, the death of any creature is for him essentially "a change in form" as the great cycles of life revolve, leaving him with the conviction that "happiness survives", and that the organic residues of mountain, rock and sand are "monuments of past delight". This primacy of happiness in his poem enjoins on him a prescription of the means to achieve it; and out of this imperative arise the central themes of health, of virtue, and ultimately of sexuality that dominate much of the poem. I believe that the modern reader will find in Cosmologia much that is applicable to our own condition and concerns as we progress through the twenty-first century. This new edition is intended as a living text not as a literary memorial.

To this end, I trust that the format of this edition makes easy an enjoyment of the poem as "plain text". I have not included Darwin's "philosophical notes" either as footnotes or as the additional notes of the original editions; neither have I included Darwin's introductory pieces, nor the three prose "Interludes" of "The Loves of the Plants". These will have to be sought in the earlier editions. In other words, Darwin's Muse is here presented very much as he accounted for his visit to the limestone caves of Derbyshire's Peak District: "I...have seen the Goddess of Minerals naked, as she lay in her inmost bowers".

The analogy is not altogether playful! The reader will find Darwin's poetry very visual, as the precision and purity of his diction articulates the forms and dynamic processes of nature and of technology. He is able to make poetry equally imaginatively out of the botanical details of plant anatomy as out of a winter landscape; the operation of Arkwright's "water-frame" or John Michell's astronomical "black hole" hypothesis. The sheer variety of his scenarios, stretching from the microcosmic speck to the macrocosmic system, is a delight in itself. Cosmologia, in its universality, is in the tradition of Geoffrey Chaucer's "Prologue" to The Canterbury Tales, and of Alexander Pope's Essay on Man; of William Shakespeare's The Tempest and John Milton's Paradise Lost; indeed echoes of the last three will be found intertextually in Darwin's poem as a prompt for us to place his individual talent alongside theirs. At this point I should like to recommend that Darwin's poetry be read aloud, since I wholly agree with Anna Seward when she judges that he succeeded in "bringing the couplet measure to a degree of sonorous perfection".

In this new edition, I have given the general title Cosmologia to the two parts of The Botanic Garden: "The Economy of Vegetation" (1791) and "The Loves of the Plants" (1789), together with "The Temple of Nature" (1803). Each of these three epics is divided into four cantos, and is roughly of equal length with the others. My purpose in doing this is to promote a reading of the poems as a sequence which recapitulates the history of the cosmos.

The first part, "The Economy of Vegetation" dramatises the birth and evolution of the universe using the early Empedoclean paradigm of the Four Elements in each of its four cantos: Fire, Earth, Water, and Air. These elements emerge as the sustainers of the "economy of vegetation" , as well as providing the chemistry with which humanity builds its technological civilisation. The builders of that industrial civilisation - Joseph Priestley, Josiah Wedgwood, James Brindley et al. - appear in their appropriate element.

The second part, "The Loves of the Plants", dramatises that crucial step in our understanding of the living world, the Linnaean taxonomy. Its classification of the vegetable kingdom is extended, by analogy but in a deeper sense naturally, to human life itself: "when a monarch or a mushroom dies". Canto One is a catalogue of floral and human sexuality; Canto Two promotes the contribution of plants to human progress in the arts and sciences; Canto Three, conversely, projects a nightmare vision of regressive human pathology; Canto Four reaffirms the prime virtues of love and sexuality.

Cosmologia's third part was originally entitled "The Origin of Society" by Darwin, but his politically vulnerable radical publisher, Joseph Johnson, favoured the uncontroversial title "The Temple of Nature". Here, Darwin's own subheadings for each canto indicate their scope: "Production of Life", "Reproduction of Life", "Progress of the Mind", and "Of Good and Evil".
This whole sequence gives us, therefore, Western science's early proto-scientific elemental model, followed by the eighteenth century's achievement, in Linnaeus,

of an empirical systema naturae, culminating in Darwin's forward-looking evolutionary scenario. The discourse of Cosmologia's progressive sequence also replaces the hierarchical "Great Chain of Being", on which both Milton and Pope had built their world-views, with the evolutionary "long line of being" which, as Darwin says, "never ends". In addition, Darwin converts - or perhaps subverts - the Miltonic Fall of Man into a crucial evolutionary stage when sexual reproduction - that "master-piece of nature" - replaced the inherently and dangerously flawed mechanism of asexual division, earlier represented, indeed, by the "hermaphroditic" Adam from the division of whose rib-cells Eve emerges. The asexual Tree of Life itself is similarly in danger of species-deterioration until floral sex follows the Fall. We can see at every level in the sequence - and this includes Darwin's modulation of his style from the concrete to the more abstract use of words and his accompanying shift from the "looser analogies, which dress out the imagery of poetry" in Parts One and Two to "the stricter ones, which form the ratiocination of philosophy" in Part Three - the functioning of Darwin's progressive model.

It is one of literary culture's greatest quirks of history that such poetry, and of such an influential figure as Erasmus Darwin, should not be readily available to the general reader. For the past two hundred years Darwin's epic poetry has been totally eclipsed by the Romantic moon of S.T.Coleridge. During the brief period between 1789 and 1798, Darwin's epic poems received critical acclaim. Horace Walpole referred to "The Loves of the Plants" as "the most lovely poetry"; Sir Walter Scott gave Darwin "a ranking among British poets of the highest class"; and Coleridge could still say of him in 1797 that "he is the first literary character in Europe", although later, in his Biographia Literaria, he claimed a very different attitude: "I remember to have compared Darwin's work to the Russian palace of ice, glittering, cold, and transitory." So the shadow of the moon was already beginning to obscure the sun of Darwin's great Enlightenment epic, and this from Coleridge (and William Wordsworth) who had begun writing in the reflected light of Darwin's poetry. Wordsworth later claimed that in his early days he suffered from an "injurious influence from the dazzling manner of Darwin". But Darwin's influence remained long enough to provide ideas for some of the Lyrical Ballads, including Coleridge's "The Rime of the Ancient Mariner". This influence is also traceable in many other Romantic literature, including the engraved work of William Blake and in the writings of both the Shelleys: Mary Shelley's Frankenstein, for example, draws on and acknowledges Darwin's theories about electricity and life. The afterglow of Darwin's influence suggests an analogy from his own writing: "[shells] are set on fire by the sun's rays, and continue for some time a slow combustion after they are withdrawn from the light".

This new edition is intended not only to celebrate the bicentenary of Darwin's death in 1802 but also to herald the end of the eclipse. Furthermore, it is intended as a tribute to the torch-bearing work of Desmond King-Hele, without whose enormous scholarship in promotion of Darwin's life and work, this edition of the poetry would not have seen the light.

DR ERASMUS DARWIN, FRS (1731-1802)

The doctor's green-gold phaeton, whose spoked wheels's

Serpentine-springs glide easily over

The unmade earth of country roads, carries
Sweetmeats, surgical instruments, mercury;

And books as guidance for a cosmic journey:
Bryant's Mythology, Linnaeus, Herschel's
Star-map, and Newton's Principia;

And words (stuttered maybe): enquiries,
Diagnoses offered with sympathy;
Witty exchanges, sarcasm occasionally
Too strong for the listener; passionate appeals
To altruism and our better nature.

And poetry: artesian well-water
Sustaining a muse who is the goddess
Of botany; the genius loci
Of a star-flower garden whose beauty fills
Every couplet. Wheels mired in mud, the car
Halts by a garden-gate, and the doctor
Strides, with offered apple-tart, towards a lass
Thinned to the bone by work and poverty.

Stuart Harris

Part One

THE ECONOMY OF VEGETATION

(An Elemental Model)

[Preamble to Canto One][1]

" Stay your rude steps! whose throbbing breasts infold
The legion-fiends of Glory, or of Gold!
Stay! whose false lips seductive simpers part,
While Cunning nestles in the harlot-heart!
For you no Dryads dress the roseate bower;
For you no Nymphs their sparkling vases pour;
Unmark'd by you, light Graces skim the green,
And hovering Cupids aim their shafts unseen.

" But Thou! whose mind the well-attemper'd ray
Of Taste and Virtue lights with purer day;
Whose finer sense each soft vibration owns
With sweet responsive sympathy of tones
(So the fair flower expands its lucid form
To meet the sun, and shuts it to the storm);
For thee my borders nurse the fragrant wreath,
My fountains murmur, and my zephyrs breathe;
Slow slides the painted snail, the gilded fly
Smooths his fine down, to charm thy curious eye;
On twinkling fins my pearly nations play,
Or win with sinuous train their trackless way;
My plumy pairs, in gay embroidery dress'd,
Form with ingenious bill the pensile nest;
To Love's sweet notes attune the listening dell,
And Echo sounds her soft symphonious shell.

" And, if with Thee some hapless Maid should stray,
Disastrous Love companion of her way,
Oh, lead her timid steps to yonder glade,
Whose arching cliffs depending alders shade.
There, as meek Evening wakes her temperate breeze,
And moon-beams glimmer through the trembling trees,

[1] Lines 1-16, 25-40, and 51-58 are adopted and adapted from Anna Seward's complimentary verses written in Darwin's botanic garden at Lichfield. [ed.]

The rills, that gurgle round, shall soothe her ear,
The weeping rocks shall number tear for tear;
There as sad Philomel, alike forlorn,
Sings to the night from her accustomed thorn,
While at sweet intervals each falling note
Sighs in the gale, and whispers round the grot,
The sister-woe shall calm her aching breast,
And softer slumbers steal her cares to rest.

" Winds of the North! restrain your icy gales,
Nor chill the bosom of these happy vales!
Hence in dark heaps, ye gathering Clouds, revolve!
Disperse, ye Lightnings! and, ye Mists, dissolve!
Hither, emerging from yon orient skies,
Botanic Goddess! bend thy radiant eyes;
O'er these soft scenes assume thy gentle reign,
Pomona, Ceres, Flora in thy train;
O'er the still dawn thy placid smile effuse,
And with thy silver sandals print the dews;
In noon's bright blaze thy vermil vest unfold,
And wave thy emerald banner starr'd with gold."

Thus spake the Genius[2] as he stepp'd along
And bade these lawns to Peace and Truth belong.
Down the steep slopes he led with modest skill
The willing pathway and the truant rill;
Stretch'd o'er the marshy vale yon willowy mound,
Where shines the lake amid the tufted ground;
Raised the young woodland, smooth'd the wavy green,
And gave to Beauty all the quiet scene.

She comes, the Goddess, through the whispering air.
Bright as the morn descends her blushing car:
Each circling wheel a wreath of flowers entwines,
And gemm'd with flowers the silken harness shines;
The golden bits with flowery studs are deck'd,
And knots of flowers the crimson reins connect;
And now on earth the silver axle rings,
And the shell sinks upon its slender springs.
Light from her airy seat the Goddess bounds,
And steps celestial press the pansied grounds.

---

[2] i.e. the Genius of the Place, Erasmus Darwin as characterised by Anna Seward in this her *exordium* [ed.]

Fair Spring advancing calls her feather'd quire,
And tunes to softer notes her laughing lyre;
Bids her gay Hours on purple pinions move,
And arms her Zephyrs with the shafts of Love.
Pleased Gnomes, ascending from their earthy beds,
Play round her graceful footsteps, as she treads;
Gay Sylphs attendant beat the fragrant air
On winnowing wings, and waft her golden hair;
Blue Nymphs emerging leave their sparkling streams,
And Fiery Forms alight from orient beams;
Musk'd in the rose's lap fresh dews they shed,
Or breathe celestial lustres round her head.
First the fine Forms her dulcet voice requires,
Which bathe or bask in elemental fires:
From each bright gem of Day's refulgent car,
From the pale sphere of every twinkling star,
From each nice pore of ocean, earth, and air,
With eye of flame the sparkling hosts repair,
Mix their gay hues, in changeful circles play,
Like motes that tenant the meridian ray.
(So the clear Lens collects with magic power
The countless glories of the midnight hour;
Stars after stars with quivering lustre fall,
And twinkling glide along the whiten'd wall.)
Pleased, as they pass she counts the glittering bands,
And stills their murmur with her waving hands;
Each listening tribe with fond expectance burns,
And now to these, and now to those, she turns.

Canto One

(The Element of Fire)

I " Nymphs of primeval Fire! your vestal train
Hung with gold-tresses o'er the vast inane,
Pierced with your silver shafts the throne of Night,
And charm'd young Nature's opening eyes with light,
When Love Divine, with brooding wings unfurl'd,
Call'd from the rude abyss the living world.
'Let there be light!' proclaim'd the Almighty Lord.
Astonish'd Chaos heard the potent word.

Through all his realms the kindling Ether[3] runs,
And the mass starts into a million suns;
Earths round each sun with quick explosions burst,
And second planets issue from the first;
Bend, as they journey with projectile force,
In bright ellipses their reluctant course;
Orbs wheel in orbs, round centres centres roll,
And form, self-balanced, one revolving Whole.
Onward they move amid their bright abode,
Space without bound, the bosom of their God!

II " Ethereal Powers! you chase the shooting stars,
Or yoke the vollied lightnings to your cars;
Cling round the aerial bow with prisms bright,
And pleased, untwist the sevenfold threads of light;
Eve's silken couch with gorgeous tints adorn,
And fire the arrowy throne of rising Morn.
Or plumed with flame in gay battalions spring
To brighter regions, borne on broader wing,
Where lighter gases, circumfused on high,
Form the vast concave of exterior sky;
With airy lens the scatter'd rays assault,
And bend the twilight round the dusky vault;
Ride, with broad eye and scintillating hair,
The rapid fire-ball through the midnight air;
Dart from the North on pale electric streams,
Fringing Night's sable robe with transient beams.
Or rein the planets in their swift careers,
Gilding with borrow'd light their twinkling spheres;
Alarm with comet-blaze the sapphire plain,
The wan stars glimmering through its silver train;
Gem the bright zodiac, stud the glowing pole,
Or give the Sun's phlogistic[4] orb to roll.

III.i " Nymphs! your fine Forms with steps impassive mock
Earth's vaulted roofs of adamantine rock;
Round her still centre tread the burning soil,
And watch the billowy lavas as they boil;

---

3 pure air, an element [JD]; non-material pervasive cosmic entity; Aristotle's 5th Element [ed.]
4 inflammatory, hot [JD]

Where, in basaltic caves imprison'd deep,
Reluctant Fires in dread suspension sleep;
Or sphere on sphere in widening waves expand,
And glad with genial[5] warmth the incumbent land.
So when the mother-bird selects their food
With curious bill, and feeds her callow brood,
Warmth from her tender heart eternal springs,
And pleased she clasps them with extended wings.

ii " You from deep cauldrons and unmeasured caves
Blow flaming airs, or pour vitrescent waves;
O'er shining oceans ray volcanic light,
Or hurl innocuous embers to the night.
While with loud shouts to Etna Heccla calls,
And Andes answers from his beacon'd walls,
Sea-wilder'd crews the mountain-stars admire,
And Beauty beams amid terrific fire.

" Thus when of old, as mystic bards presume,
Huge Cyclops dwelt in Etna's rocky womb,
On thundering anvils rung their loud alarms,
And leagued with Vulcan forged immortal arms,
Descending Venus sought the dark abode,
And sooth'd the labours of the grisly god.
While frowning Loves the threatening falchion[6] wield,
And tittering Graces peep behind the shield,
With jointed mail their fairy limbs o'erwhelm,
Or nod with pausing step the plumed helm,
With radiant eye she view'd the boiling ore,
Heard undismay'd the breathing bellows roar,
Admired their sinewy arms and shoulders bare,
And ponderous hammers lifted high in air,
With smiles celestial bless'd their dazzled sight,
And Beauty blazed amid infernal night.

IV " Effulgent Maids! you round deciduous[7] day,
Tressed with soft beams, your glittering bands array;
On Earth's cold bosom, as the sun retires,
Confine with folds of air the lingering fires;
O'er Eve's pale forms diffuse phosphoric light,
And deck with lambent flames the shrine of Night.

---

[5] contributing to propagation, natural [JD]
[6] a kind of short crooked sword [JD]
[7] declining [ed.]

So, warm'd and kindled by meridian skies,
And view'd in darkness with dilated eyes,
Bologna's chalks with faint ignition blaze,
Beccari's shells emit prismatic rays.
So to the sacred Sun in Memnon's fane
Spontaneous concords quired the matin strain;
Touch'd by his orient beam, responsive rings
The living lyre, and vibrates all its strings;
Accordant aisles the tender tones prolong,
And holy echoes swell the adoring song.

" You with light gas the lamps nocturnal feed,
Which dance and glimmer o'er the marshy mead;
Shine round Calendula at twilight hours,
And tip with silver all her saffron flowers;
Warm on her mossy couch the radiant worm;
Guard from cold dews her love-illumined form;
From leaf to leaf conduct the virgin light,
Star of the earth, and diamond of the night.
You bid in air the tropic beetle burn,
And fill with golden flame his winged urn;
Or gild the surge with insect-sparks, that swarm
Round the bright oar, the kindling prow alarm;
Or arm in waves, electric in his ire,
The dread Gymnotus with ethereal fire:
Onward his course with waving tail he helms,
And mimic lightnings scare the watery realms.
So, when with bristling plumes the bird of Jove
Vindictive leaves the argent fields above,
Borne on broad wings the guilty world he awes,
And grasps the lightning in his shining claws.

V.i " Nymphs! your soft smiles uncultur'd man subdued,
And charm'd the savage from his native wood;
You, while amazed his hurrying hordes retire
From the fell havoc of devouring fire,
Taught - the first art! - with piny rods to raise
By quick attrition[8] the domestic blaze,
Fan with soft breath, with kindling leaves provide,
And list[9] the dread destroyer on his side.
So, with bright wreath of serpent-tresses crown'd,
Severe in beauty, young Medusa frown'd;

---

[8] rubbing one stick against another [JD]
[9] to enlist soldiers [JD]

Erewhile subdued, round Wisdom's Aegis[10] roll'd,
Hiss'd the dread snakes, and flamed in burnish'd gold;
Flash'd on her brandish'd arm the immortal shield,
And terror lighten'd o'er the dazzled field.

ii " Nymphs! you disjoin, unite, condense, expand,
And give new wonders to the chemist's hand;
On tepid clouds of rising steam aspire,
Or fix in sulphur all its solid fire;
With boundless spring elastic airs unfold,
Or fill the fine vacuities of gold;
With sudden flash vitrescent sparks reveal,
By fierce collision from the flint and steel;
Or mark with shining letters Kunkel's name
In the pale phosphor's self-consuming flame.
So the chaste heart of some enchanted maid
Shines with insidious light, by love betray'd.
Round her pale bosom plays the young Desire,
And slow she wastes by self-consuming fire.

iii " You taught mysterious Bacon to explore
Metallic veins, and part the dross from ore;
With sylvan coal in whirling mills combine
The crystall'd nitre, and the sulphurous mine;
Through wiry nets the black diffusion strain,
And close an airy ocean in a grain.
Pent in dark chambers of cylindric brass,
Slumbers in grim repose the sooty mass;
Lit by the brilliant spark, from grain to grain
Runs the quick fire along the kindling train;
On the pain'd ear-drum bursts the sudden crash,
Starts the red flame, and Death pursues the flash.
Fear's feeble hand directs the fiery darts,
And Strength and Courage yield to chemic arts;
Guilt with pale brow the mimic thunder owns,
And tyrants tremble on their blood-stain'd thrones.

VI " Nymphs! you erewhile on simmering cauldrons play'd,
And call'd delighted Savery to your aid;
Bade round the youth explosive steam aspire
In gathering clouds, and wing'd the wave with fire;
Bade with cold streams the quick expansion stop,
And sunk the immense of vapour to a drop.

---

[10] shield belonging to Pallas Athene featuring 'a Gorgon whom Pallas slew' [JD]

Press'd by the ponderous air the piston falls
Resistless, sliding through its iron walls;
Quick moves the balanced beam, of giant birth,
Wields his large limbs, and nodding shakes the earth.

" The Giant-power from earth's remotest caves
Lifts with strong arm her dark reluctant waves;
Each cavern'd rock and hidden den explores,
Drags her dark coals, and digs her shining ores.
Next, in close cells of ribbed oak confined,
Gale after gale, he crowds the struggling wind:
The imprison'd storms through brazen nostrils roar,
Fan the white flame, and fuse the sparkling ore.
Here high in air the rising stream he pours
To clay-built cisterns, or to lead-lined towers;
Fresh through a thousand pipes the wave distils,
And thirsty cities drink the exuberant rills.
There the vast mill-stone with inebriate whirl
On trembling floors his forceful fingers twirl,
Whose flinty teeth the golden harvests grind,
Feast without blood! and nourish human-kind.

" Now his hard hands on Mona's rifted crest,
Bosom'd in rock, her azure ores arrest;
With iron lips his rapid rollers seize
The lengthening bars, in thin expansion squeeze;
Descending screws with ponderous fly-wheels wound
The tawny plates, the new medallions round;
Hard dies of steel the cupreous circles cramp,
And with quick fall his massy hammers stamp.
The Harp, the Lily and the Lion join,
And George and Britain guard the sterling coin.

" Soon shall thy arm, unconquer'd Steam! afar
Drag the slow barge, or drive the rapid car;
Or on wide-waving wings expanded bear
The flying-chariot through the fields of air.
Fair crews triumphant, leaning from above,
Shall wave their fluttering kerchiefs as they move;
Or warrior-bands alarm the gaping crowd,
And armies shrink beneath the shadowy cloud.

" So mighty Hercules o'er many a clime
Waved his vast mace in Virtue's cause sublime:

Unmeasured strength with early art combined,
Awed, served, protected, and amazed mankind.
First, two dread snakes at Juno's vengeful nod
Climb'd round the cradle of the sleeping god;
Waked by the shrilling hiss, and rustling sound,
And shrieks of fair attendants trembling round,
Their gasping throats with clenching hands he holds,
And Death untwists their convoluted folds.
Next in red torrents from her sevenfold heads
Fell Hydra's blood on Lerna's lake he sheds;
Grasps Achelous with resistless force,
And drags the roaring river to his course;
Binds with loud bellowing and with hideous yell
The monster bull, and threefold dog of hell.

" Then, where Nemea's howling forests wave,
He drives the lion to his dusky cave:
Seized by the throat the growling fiend disarms,
And tears his gaping jaws with sinewy arms;
Lifts proud Anteus from his mother-plains,
And with strong grasp the struggling giant strains:
Back falls his fainting head and clammy hair,
Writhe his weak limbs, and flits his life in air.
By steps reverted o'er the blood-dropp'd fen,
He tracks huge Cacus to his murderous den,
Where, breathing flames through brazen lips, he fled,
And shakes the rock-roof'd cavern o'er his head.

" Last, with wide arms the solid earth he tears,
Piles rock on rock, on mountain mountain rears;
Heaves up huge Abyla on Afric's sand;
Crowns with high Calpe Europe's salient strand;
Crests with opposing towers the splendid scene,
And pours from urns immense the sea between.
Loud o'er her whirling flood Charybdis roars;
Affrighted Scylla bellows round her shores;
Vesuvio groans through all his echoing caves,
And Etna thunders o'er the insurgent waves.

VII.i " Nymphs! your fine hands ethereal floods amass
From the warm cushion, and the whirling glass;
Beard the bright cylinder with golden wire,
And circumfuse the gravitating fire.
Cold from each point cerulean lustres gleam,
Or shoot in air the scintillating stream.

So, borne on brazen talons, watch'd of old
The sleepless dragon o'er his fruits of gold;
Bright beam'd his scales, his eye-balls blazed with ire,
And his wide nostrils breath'd inchanted fire.

" You bid gold-leaves, in crystal lanterns held,
Approach attracted, and recede repell'd;
While paper-nymphs instinct with motion rise,
And dancing fauns the admiring sage surprise.
Or, if on wax some fearless beauty stand,
And touch the sparkling rod with graceful hand,
Through her fine limbs the mimic lightnings dart,
And flames innocuous eddy round her heart.
O'er her fair brow the kindling lustres glare,
Blue rays diverging from her bristling hair,
While some fond youth the kiss ethereal sips,
And soft fires issue from their meeting lips.
So round the virgin saint in silver streams
The holy halo shoots its arrowy beams.

" You crowd in coated jars the denser fire,
Pierce the thin glass, and fuse the blazing wire;
Or dart the red flash through the circling band
Of youths and timorous damsels, hand in hand:
Starts the quick Ether through the fibre-trains
Of dancing arteries, and of tingling veins,
Goads each fine nerve, with new sensation thrill'd;
Bends the reluctant limbs with power unwill'd.
Palsy's cold hands the fierce concussion own,
And Life clings trembling on her tottering throne.
So from dark clouds the playful lightning springs,
Rives the firm oak, or prints the fairy-rings.

ii " Nymphs! on that day you shed from lucid eyes
Celestial tears, and breathed ethereal sighs!
When Richman rear'd, by fearless haste betray'd,
The wiry rod in Nieva's fatal shade;
Clouds o'er the sage with fringed skirts succeed,
Flash follows flash, the warning corks recede;
Near and more near he eyed with fond amaze
The silver streams, and watch'd the sapphire blaze;
Then burst the steel, the dart electric sped,
And the bold sage lay number'd with the dead!
Nymphs! on that day you shed from lucid eyes
Celestial tears, and breathed ethereal sighs!

iii “ You led your Franklin to your glazed retreats,
Your air-built castles, and your silken seats;
Bade his bold arm invade the lowering sky,
And seize the tiptoe lightnings, ere they fly;
O’er the young sage your mystic mantle spread,
And wreath’d the crown electric round his head.
Thus when on wanton wing intrepid Love
Snatch’d the raised lightning from the arm of Jove,
Quick o’er his knee the triple bolt he bent,
The cluster’d darts and forky arrows rent,
Snapp’d with illumined hands each flaming shaft;
His tingling fingers shook, and stamp’d and laugh’d.
Bright o’er the floor the scatter’d fragments blazed,
And gods retreating trembled as they gazed.
The immortal sire, indulgent to his child,
Bow’d his ambrosial locks, and Heaven relenting smiled.

VIII “ When air’s pure essence joins the vital flood,
And with phosphoric acid dyes the blood,
Your virgin trains the transient heat dispart,
And lead the soft combustion round the heart.
Life’s holy lamp with fires successive feed,
From the crown’d forehead to the prostrate weed,
From Earth’s proud realms to all that swim or sweep
The yielding ether or tumultuous deep.
You swell the bulb beneath the heaving lawn,
Brood the live seed, unfold the bursting spawn;
Nurse with soft lap, and warm with fragrant breath
The embryon panting in the arms of Death;
Youth’s vivid eye with living light adorn,
And fire the rising blush of Beauty’s golden morn.

“ Thus when the Egg of Night, on Chaos hurl’d,
Burst, and disclosed the cradle of the world,
First from the gaping shell refulgent sprung
Immortal Love, his bow celestial strung;
O’er the wide waste his gaudy wings unfold,
Beam his soft smiles, and wave his curls of gold;
With silver darts he pierced the kindling frame,
And lit with torch divine the ever-living flame.”

IX The Goddess paused, admired with conscious pride
The effulgent legions marshall’d by her side:

Forms sphered in fire with trembling light array'd,
Ens[11] without weight, and substance without shade;
And, while tumultuous joy her bosom warms,
Waves her white hand, and calls her hosts to arms.

" Unite, illustrious Nymphs! your radiant powers;
Call from their long repose the Vernal Hours;
Wake with soft touch, with rosy hands unbind
The struggling pinions of the western Wind;
Chafe his wan cheeks, his ruffled plumes repair,
And wring the rain-drops from his tangled hair.
Blaze round each frosted rill, or stagnant wave,
And charm the Naiad from her silent cave,
Where, shrined in ice, like Niobe she mourns,
And clasps with hoary arms her empty urns.
Call your bright myriads, trooping from afar,
With beamy helms and glittering shafts of war.
In phalanx firm the Fiend of Frost assail,
Break his white towers, and pierce his crystal mail;
To Zembla's moon-bright coasts the tyrant bear,
And chain him howling to the Northern Bear.

" So, when enormous Grampus, issuing forth
From the pale regions of the icy North,
Waves his broad tail, and opes his ribbed mouth,
And seeks on winnowing fin the breezy South,
From towns deserted rush the breathless hosts,
Swarm round the hills, and darken all the coasts.
Boats follow boats along the shouting tides,
And spears and javelins pierce his blubbery sides:
Now the bold sailor, raised on pointed toe,
Whirls the wing'd harpoon on the slimy foe.
Quick sinks the monster in his oozy bed,
The blood-stain'd surges circling o'er his head;
Steers to the frozen pole his wonted track,
And bears the iron tempest on his back.

X " On wings of flame, ethereal Virgins! sweep
O'er earth's fair bosom and complacent deep,
Where dwell my vegetative realms benumb'd,
In buds imprison'd, or in bulbs intomb'd.

[11] any being or existence [JD]

Pervade, pellucid Forms! their cold retreat;
Ray from bright urns your viewless floods of heat;
From earth's deep wastes electric torrents pour,
Or shed from heaven the scintillating shower.
Pierce the dull root, relax its fibre-trains,
Thaw the thick blood, which lingers in its veins;
Melt with warm breath the fragrant gums, that bind
The expanding foliage in its scaly rind.
And, as in air the laughing leaflets play
And turn their shining bosoms to the ray,
Nymphs! with sweet smile each opening flower invite,
And on its damask eyelids pour the light.

" So shall my pines, Canadian wilds that shade,
Where no bold step has pierc'd the tangled glade;
High-towering palms, that part the southern flood
With shadowy isles and continents of wood;
Oaks, whose broad antlers crest Britannia's plain,
Or bear her thunders o'er the conquer'd main,
Shout, as you pass, inhale the genial skies,
And bask and brighten in your beamy eyes;
Bow their white heads, admire the changing clime,
Shake from their candied trunks the tinkling rime;
With bursting buds their wrinkled barks adorn,
And wed the timorous floret to her thorn;
Deep strike their roots, their lengthening tops revive,
And all my world of foliage wave, alive.

" Thus with hermetic art the adept combines
The royal acid with cobaltic mines;
Marks with quick pen, in lines unseen portray'd,
The blushing mead, green dell, and dusky glade;
Shades with pellucid clouds the tintless field,
And all the future group exists conceal'd.
Till waked by fire the dawning tablet glows,
Green springs the herb, the purple floret blows,
Hills, vales, and woods in bright succession rise,
And all the living landscape charms his eyes.

XI " With crest of gold should sultry Sirius glare,
And with his kindling tresses scorch the air,
With points of flame the shafts of Summer arm,
And burn the beauties he designs to warm.
(So erst when Jove his oath extorted mourn'd,
And clad in glory to the Fair return'd,

While Loves at forky bolts their torches light,
And resting lightnings gild the car of Night,
His blazing form the dazzled maid admired,
Met with fond lips, and in his arms expired.)
Nymphs! on light pinions lead your banner'd hosts
High o'er the cliffs of Orkney's gulfy coasts;
Leave on your left the red volcanic light
Which Heccla lifts amid the dusky night;
Mark on the right the Dofrine's snow-capt brow,
Where whirling Maelstrome roars and foams below;
Watch, with unmoving eye, where Cepheus bends
His triple crown, his sceptred hand extends;
Where studs Cassiope with stars unknown
Her golden hair, and gems her sapphire zone[12];
Where with vast convolution Draco holds
The ecliptic axis in his scaly folds,
O'er half the skies his neck enormous rears,
And with immense meanders parts the Bears;
Onward the kindred Bears with footstep rude
Dance round the Pole, pursuing and pursued.

"There, in her azure coif[13] and starry stole,
Grey Twilight sits, and rules the slumbering Pole;
Bends the pale moon-beams round the sparkling coast,
And strews with livid hands eternal frost.
There, Nymphs! alight, array your dazzling powers,
With sudden march alarm the torpid hours;
On ice-built isles expand a thousand sails, 529
Hinge the strong helms, and catch the frozen gales; [a]
The winged rocks to feverish climates guide, [b][14]
Where fainting Zephyrs pant upon the tide;
Pass, where to Ceuta Calpe's[15] thunder roars,
And answering echoes shake the kindred shores;
Pass, where with palmy plumes Canary smiles,
And in her silver girdle binds her isles;
Onward where Niger's dusky Naiad laves
A thousand kingdoms with prolific waves,
Or leads o'er golden sands her threefold train
In steamy channels to the fervid main,

---

12 girdle [JD]
13 a head dress, a woman's cap [JD]
14 This couplet is mis-numbered in the 1791 edition. [ed.]
15 The Strait of Gibralter has Ceuta on its southern and Calpe on its northern shore. [ed.]

While swarthy nations crowd the sultry coast,
Drink the fresh breeze, and hail the floating frost.
Nymphs! veil'd in mist, the melting treasures steer,
And cool with arctic snows the tropic year.
So from the burning Line by monsoons driven,
Clouds sail in squadrons o'er the darken'd heaven;
Wide wastes of sand the gelid gales pervade,
And ocean cools beneath the moving shade.

XII " Should Solstice, stalking through the sickening bowers,
Suck the warm dew-drops, lap the falling showers,
Kneel with parch'd lip, and bending from its brink
From dripping palm the scanty river drink,
Nymphs! o'er the soil ten thousand points erect,
And high in air the electric flame collect.
Soon shall dark mists with self-attraction shroud
The blazing day, and sail in wilds of cloud:
Each silvery flower the streams aerial quaff,
Bow her sweet head, and infant Harvest laugh.

" Thus when Elijah mark'd from Carmel's brow
In bright expanse the briny flood below,
Roll'd his red eyes amid the scorching air,
Smote his firm breast, and breathed his ardent prayer,
High in the midst a massy altar stood,
And slaughter'd offerings press'd the piles of wood;
While Israel's chiefs the sacred hill surround,
And famish'd armies crowd the dusty ground;
While proud Idolatry was leagued with dearth,
And wither'd Famine swept the desert earth,
'Oh! mighty Lord! thy woe-worn servant hear,
Who calls thy name in agony of prayer;
Thy fanes dishonour'd, and thy prophets slain;
Lo! I alone survive of all thy train!
Oh send from heaven thy sacred fire, and pour
O'er the parch'd land the salutary shower.
So shall thy priest thy erring flock recall,
And speak in thunder, "Thou art Lord of all" ',
He cried and, kneeling on the mountain-sands,
Stretch'd high in air his supplicating hands.
Descending flames the dusky shrine illume,
Fire the wet wood, the sacred bull consume;
Wing'd from the sea the gathering mists arise,
And floating waters darken all the skies;
The king with shifted reins his chariot bends,
And wide o'er earth the airy flood descends;

With mingling cries dispersing hosts applaud,
And shouting nations own the living God."

The Goddess ceased; the exulting tribes obey,
Start from the soil, and win their airy way.
The vaulted skies with streams of transient rays
Shine, as they pass, and earth and ocean blaze.
So from fierce wars when lawless monarchs cease,
Or liberty returns with laurell'd peace,
Bright fly the sparks, the colour'd lustres burn,
Flash follows flash, and flame-wing'd circles turn;
Blue serpents sweep along the dusky air,
Imp'd[16] by long trains of scintillating hair;
Red rockets rise, loud cracks are heard on high,
And showers of stars rush headlong from the sky,
Burst, as in silver lines they hiss along,
And the quick flash unfolds the gazing throng.

End of Canto One

---

[16] lengthened [JD]

Canto Two

(The Element of Earth)

And now the Goddess with attention sweet
Turns to the Gnomes that circle round her feet;
Orb within orb approach the marshall'd trains,
And pigmy legions darken all the plains;
Thrice shout with silver tones the applauding bands,
Bow, ere she speaks, and clap their fairy hands.
So the tall grass, when noon-tide zephyr blows,
Bends its green blades in undulating rows;
Wide o'er the fields the billowy tumult spreads,
And rustling harvests bow their golden heads.

I " Gnomes! your bright forms, presiding at her birth,
Clung in fond squadrons round the new-born Earth:
When high in Ether, with explosion dire,
From the deep craters of his realms of fire,
The whirling Sun this ponderous planet hurl'd,
And gave the astonish'd void another world;
When from its vaporous air, condensed by cold,
Descending torrents into ocean roll'd;
And fierce attraction with relentless force
Bent the reluctant wanderer to its course.
Where yet the Bull with diamond-eye adorns
The spring's fair forehead, and with golden horns;
Where yet the Lion climbs the ethereal plain,
And shakes the Summer from his radiant mane;
Where Libra lifts her airy arm, and weighs,
Poised in her silver balance, nights and days;
With paler lustres where Aquarius burns,
And showers the still snow from his hoary urns;
Your ardent troops pursued the flying sphere,
Circling the starry girdle of the year;
While sweet vicissitudes of day and clime
Mark'd the new annals of enascent time.

II " You trod with printless step Earth's tender globe,
While Ocean wrapp'd it in his azure robe;
Beneath his waves her hardening strata spread;
Raised her primeval islands from his bed;
Stretch'd her wide lawns and sunk her winding dells,
And deck'd her shores with corals, pearls, and shells.

" O'er those blest isles no ice-crown'd mountains tower'd,
No lightnings darted, and no tempests lower'd;
Soft fell the vesper-drops, condensed below,
Or bent in air the rain-refracted bow;
Sweet breathed the zephyrs, just perceiv'd and lost,
And brineless billows only kiss'd the coast;
Round the bright zodiac danced the Vernal Hours,
And Peace, the cherub, dwelt in mortal bowers!

" So young Dione, nursed beneath the waves,
And rock'd by Nereids in their coral caves,
Charm'd the blue sisterhood with playful wiles,
Lisp'd her sweet tones, and tried her tender smiles.
Then, on her beryl throne by Tritons borne,
Bright rose the goddess like the star of morn,
When with soft fires the milky dawn he leads,
And wakes to life and love the laughing meads.
With rosy fingers, as uncurl'd they hung
Round her fair brow, her golden locks she wrung;
O'er the smooth surge on silver sandals stood,
And look'd enchantment on the dazzled flood.
The bright drops, rolling from her lifted arms,
In slow meanders wander o'er her charms,
Seek round her snowy neck their lucid track,
Pearl her white shoulders, gem her ivory back,
Round her fine waist and swelling bosom swim,
And star with glittering brine each crystal limb.
The immortal form enamour'd Nature hail'd,
And Beauty blazed to heaven and earth, unveil'd.

III " You! who then, kindling after many an age,
Saw with new fires the first volcano rage,
O'er smouldering heaps of livid sulphur swell
At Earth's firm centre, and distend her shell;
Saw at each opening cleft the furnace glow,
And seas rush headlong on the gulfs below.
Gnomes! how you shriek'd! when through the troubled air
Roar'd the fierce din of elemental war;
When rose the continents, and sunk the main,
And Earth's huge sphere exploding burst in twain.
Gnomes! how you gazed! when from her wounded side,
Where now the South-Sea heaves its waste of tide,
Rose on swift wheels the Moon's refulgent car,
Circling the solar orb, a sister-star,
Dimpled with vales, with shining hills emboss'd,
And roll'd round Earth her airless realms of frost.

Gnomes! how you trembled with the dreadful force,
When Earth recoiling stagger'd from her course;
When, as her Line in slower circles spun,
And her shock'd axis nodded from the Sun,
With dreadful march the accumulated main
Swept her vast wrecks of mountain, vale, and plain;
And, while new tides their shouting floods unite
And hail their Queen, fair regent of the night,
Chain'd to one centre whirl'd the kindred spheres,
And mark'd with lunar cycles solar years.

IV **" Gnomes! you then bade dissolving shells distil**
From the loose summits of each shatter'd hill;
To each fine pore and dark interstice flow,
And fill with liquid chalk the mass below.
Whence sparry forms in dusky caverns gleam
With borrow'd light, and twice refract the beam;
While in white beds congealing rocks beneath
Court the nice chisel and desire to breathe.

" Hence wearied Hercules in marble rears
His languid limbs, and rests a thousand years;
Still, as he leans, shall young Antinous please
With careless grace and unaffected ease;
Onward with loftier step Apollo spring,
And launch the unerring arrow from the string;
In Beauty's bashful form, the veil unfurl'd,
Ideal Venus win the gazing world.
Hence on Roubiliac's tomb shall Fame sublime
Wave her triumphant wings and conquer Time;
Long with soft touch shall Damer's chisel charm,
With grace delight us, and with beauty warm;
Foster's fine form shall hearts unborn engage,
And Melbourn's smile enchant another age.

V. i **" Gnomes! you then taught transuding[17] dews to pass**
Through time-fall'n woods and root-inwove morass
Age after age; and with filtration fine
Dispart, from earths and sulphurs, the saline.

" Hence with diffusive salt old Ocean steeps
His emerald shallows and his sapphire deeps.

[17] passing through in vapour [JD]

Oft in wide lakes, around their warmer brim,
In hollow pyramids the crystals swim;
Or, fused by earth-born fires, in cubic blocks
Shoot their white forms, and harden into rocks.
Thus, cavern'd round in Cracow's mighty mines,
With crystal walls a gorgeous city shines:
Scoop'd in the briny rock long streets extend
Their hoary course, and glittering domes ascend;
Down the bright steeps, emerging into day,
Impetuous fountains burst their headlong way,
O'er milk-white vales in ivory channels spread,
And wondering seek their subterraneous bed.
Form'd in pellucid salt with chisel nice,
The pale lamp glimmering through the sculptured ice,
With wild reverted eyes fair Lotta stands
And spreads to Heaven, in vain, her glassy hands;
Cold dews condense upon her pearly breast
And the big tear rolls lucid down her vest.
Far gleaming o'er the town, transparent fanes
Rear their white towers and wave their golden vanes;
Long lines of lustres pour their trembling rays,
And the bright vault returns the mingled blaze.

ii " Hence orient nitre owes its sparkling birth,
And with prismatic crystals gems the earth,
O'er tottering domes in filmy foliage crawls,
Or frosts with branching plumes the mouldering walls.
As woos Azotic Gas[18] the virgin Air,
And veils in crimson clouds the yielding Fair,
Indignant Fire the treacherous courtship flies,
Waves his light wing and mingles with the skies.

" So Beauty's Goddess, warm with new desire,
Left, on her silver wheels, the God of Fire;
Her faithless charms to fiercer Mars resign'd,
Met with fond lips, with wanton arms intwined.
Indignant Vulcan eyed the parting Fair,
And watch'd with jealous step the guilty pair;
O'er his broad neck a wiry net he flung,
Quick as he strode the tinkling meshes rung;
Fine as the spider's flimsy thread he wove
The immortal toil to lime illicit love:

---

18 i.e. nitrogen [ed.]

Steel were the knots, and steel the twisted thong,
Ring link'd in ring, indissolubly strong.
On viewless hooks along the fretted roof
He hung, unseen, the inextricable woof.
Quick start the springs, the webs pellucid spread,
And lock the embracing lovers on their bed.
Fierce with loud taunts vindictive Vulcan springs,
Tries all the bolts, and tightens all the strings,
Shakes with incessant shouts the bright abodes,
Claps his rude hands, and calls the festive gods.
With spreading palms the alarmed Goddess tries
To veil her beauties from celestial eyes,
Writhes her fair limbs, the slender ringlets strains,
And bids her Loves untie the obdurate chains.
Soft swells her panting bosom, as she turns,
And her flush'd cheek with brighter blushes burns.
Majestic grief the Queen of Heaven avows,
And chaste Minerva hides her helmed brows;
Attendant Nymphs with bashful eyes askance
Steal of intangled Mars a transient glance;
Surrounding gods the circling nectar quaff,
Gaze on the Fair, and envy as they laugh.

iii " Hence dusky Iron sleeps in dark abodes,
And ferny foliage nestles in the nodes;
Till with wide lungs the panting bellows blow,
And waked by fire the glittering torrents flow.
Quick whirls the wheel, the ponderous hammer falls,
Loud anvils ring amid the trembling walls;
Strokes follow strokes, the sparkling ingot shines,
Flows the red slag, the lengthening bar refines;
Cold waves, immersed, the glowing mass congeal,
And turn to adamant the hissing Steel.

" Last, Michell's hands, with touch of potent charm,
The polish'd rods with powers magnetic arm;
With points directed to the polar stars
In one long line extend the temper'd bars;
Then thrice and thrice with steady eye he guides,
And o'er the adhesive train the magnet slides;
The obedient Steel with living instinct moves,
And veers forever to the Pole it loves.

" Hail, adamantine Steel! magnetic lord!
King of the prow, the plowshare, and the sword!

True to the Pole, by thee the pilot guides
His steady helm amid the struggling tides,
Braves with broad sail the immeasurable sea,
Cleaves the dark air, and asks no star but thee.
By thee the plowshare rends the matted plain,
Inhumes in level rows the living grain;
Intrusive forests quit the cultured ground,
And Ceres laughs with golden fillets crown'd.
O'er restless realms, when scowling Discord flings
Her snakes, and loud the din of battle rings,
Expiring Strength and vanquish'd Courage feel
Thy arm resistless, adamantine Steel!

iv " Hence in fine streams diffusive acids flow,
Or wing'd with fire o'er Earth's fair bosom blow;
Transmute to glittering flints her chalky lands,
Or sink on ocean's bed in countless sands.
Hence silvery selenite her crystal moulds,
And soft asbestos smooths his silky folds;
His cubic forms phosphoric fluor prints,
Or rays in spheres his amethystine tints;
Soft cobweb-clouds transparent onyx spreads,
And playful agates weave their colour'd threads;
Gay pictured mochoes[19] glow with landscape dyes,
And changeful opals roll their lucid eyes;
Blue lambent light around the sapphire plays,
Bright rubies blush, and living diamonds blaze.

" Thus, for attractive Earth, inconstant Jove
Mask'd in new shapes forsook his realms above.
First her sweet eyes his eagle-form beguiles,
And Hebe feeds him with ambrosial smiles;
Next the changed god a cygnet's down assumes,
And playful Leda smoothes his glossy plumes;
Then glides a silver serpent, treacherous guest!
And fair Olympia folds him in her breast;
Now lows a milk-white bull on Afric's strand,
And crops with dancing head the daisy'd land.
With rosy wreaths Europa's hand adorns
His fringed forehead, and his pearly horns;
Light on his back the sportive damsel bounds,
And pleased he moves along the flowery grounds;

[19] stones nearly related to the agate kind, of a clear horny grey, with delineations representing mosses [JD]

Bears with slow step his beauteous prize aloof,
Dips in the lucid flood his ivory hoof,
Then wets his velvet knees, and wading laves
His silky sides amid the dimpling waves.
While her fond train with beckoning hands deplore,
Strain their blue eyes, and shriek along the shore,
Beneath her robe she draws her snowy feet,
And, half-reclining on her ermine seat,
Round his raised neck her radiant arms she throws,
And rests her fair cheek on his curled brows;
Her yellow tresses wave on wanton gales,
And high in air her azure mantle sails.
Onward he moves, applauding Cupids guide,
And skim on shooting wing the shining tide;
Emerging Tritons leave their coral caves,
Sound their loud conchs[20] and smooth the circling waves,
Surround the timorous Beauty as she swims,
And gaze enamour'd on her silver limbs.
Now Europe's shadowy shores with loud acclaim
Hail the fair fugitive and shout her name;
Soft echoes warble, whispering forests nod,
And conscious Nature owns the present god.
Changed from the bull, the rapturous god assumes
Immortal youth, with glow celestial blooms,
With lenient words her virgin fears disarms,
And clasps the yielding Beauty in his arms.
Whence kings and heroes own illustrious birth:
Guards of mankind and demigods on Earth.

VI. i “ Gnomes! as you pass'd beneath the labouring soil,
The guards and guides of Nature's chemic toil,
You saw, deep-sepulchred in dusky realms,
Which Earth's rock-ribbed ponderous vault o'erwhelms,
With self-born fires the mass fermenting glow,
And flame-wing'd sulphurs quit the earths below.

“ Hence ductile clays in wide expansion spread,
Soft as the cygnet's down their snow-white bed;
With yielding flakes successive forms reveal,
And change obedient to the whirling wheel.

“ First China's sons, with early art elate,
Form'd the gay tea-pot and the pictured plate;

---

20 pronounced 'conks' [ed.]

Saw with illumined brow and dazzled eyes
In the red stove vitrescent colours rise;
Speck'd her tall beakers with enamell'd stars,
Her monster-josses and gigantic jars;
Smear'd her huge dragons with metallic hues,
With golden purples and cobaltic blues;
Bade on wide hills her porcelain castles glare,
And glazed pagodas tremble in the air.

" Etruria! next beneath thy magic hands
Glides the quick wheel, the plastic clay expands.
Nerved with fine touch, thy fingers (as it turns)
Mark the nice bounds of vases, ewers, and urns;
Round each fair form in lines immortal trace
Uncopied Beauty and ideal Grace.

" Gnomes! as you now dissect with hammers fine
The granite-rock, the noduled flint calcine;
Grind with strong arm, the circling chertz betwixt,
Your pure Kao-lins [21]and Pe-tun-tses[22] mixt;
O'er each red saggar's[23] burning cave preside,
The keen eyed Fire-Nymphs blazing by your side;
And pleased on Wedgwood ray your partial smile:
A new Etruria decks Britannia's isle.
Charm'd by your touch, the flint liquescent pours
Through finer sieves and falls in whiter showers;
Charm'd by your touch, the kneaded clay refines,
The biscuit hardens, the enamel shines;
Each nicer mould a softer feature drinks,
The bold Cameo speaks, the soft Intaglio thinks.

" To call the pearly drops from Pity's eye,
Or stay Despair's disanimating sigh,
Whether, O friend of art! the gem you mould,
Rich with new taste, with ancient virtue bold,
Form the poor fetter'd slave, on bended knee
From Britain's sons imploring to be free;
Or with fair Hope the brightening scenes improve,
And cheer the dreary wastes at Sydney-cove;
Or bid Mortality rejoice and mourn
O'er the fine forms on Portland's mystic urn.

---

[21] china clay [ed.]
[22] feldspar used in making Chinese porcelain [ed.]
[23] clay container for pottery used during the process of firing [ed.]

" Here, by fallen columns and disjoin'd arcades,
On mouldering stones, beneath deciduous shades,
Sits Humankind in hieroglyphic state,
Serious, and pondering on their changeful state;
While, with inverted torch and swimming eyes,
Sinks the fair shade of Mortal Life, and dies.
There, the pale ghost through death's wide portal bends
His timid feet, the dusky steep descends;
With smiles assuasive Love Divine invites,
Guides on broad wing, with torch uplifted lights;
Immortal Life, her hand extending, courts
The lingering form, his tottering step supports;
Leads on to Pluto's realms the dreary way,
And gives him trembling to Elysian day.
Beneath, in sacred robes the Priestess dress'd,
The coif close-hooded, and the fluttering vest,
With pointing finger guides the initiate youth,
Unweaves the many-colour'd veil of Truth,
Drives the profane from Mystery's bolted door;
And Silence guards the Eleusinian lore.

" Whether, O friend of art! your gems derive
Fine forms from Greece, and fabled gods revive;
Or bid from modern life the Portrait breathe,
And bind round Honour's brow the laurel wreath;
Buoyant shall sail, with Fame's historic page,
Each fair medallion o'er the wrecks of age;
Nor Time shall mar; nor steel, nor fire, nor rust
Touch the hard polish of the immortal bust.

ii " Hence sable coal his massy couch extends,
And stars of gold the sparkling pyrite blends;
Hence dull-eyed naptha pours his pitchy streams,
And jet uncolour'd drinks the solar beams;
Bright amber shines on his electric throne,
And adds ethereal[24] lustres to his own.

" Led by the phosphor-light, with daring tread
Immortal Franklin sought the fiery bed
Where, nursed in night, incumbent Tempest shrouds
The seeds of Thunder in circumfluent clouds,
Besieged with iron points his airy cell,
And pierced the monsters slumbering in the shell.

---

[24] i.e. derived from the ether (see Canto One, footnote 3) [ed.]

" So, borne on sounding pinions to the west,
When tyrant-power had built his eagle nest;
While from his eyry shriek'd the famish'd brood,
Clench'd their sharp claws, and champ'd their beaks for blood,
Immortal Franklin watch'd the callow[25] crew,
And stabb'd the struggling vampires ere they flew.
The patriot-flame with quick contagion ran,
Hill lighted hill, and man electrised man;
Her heroes slain awhile Columbia mourn'd,
And crown'd with laurels Liberty return'd.

" The warrior Liberty with bending sails
Helm'd his bold course to fair Hibernia's vales.
Firm as he steps along the shouting lands,
Lo! Truth and Virtue range their radiant bands;
Sad Superstition wails her empire torn,
Art plies his oar, and Commerce pours her horn.

" Long had the Giant-form on Gallia's plains
Inglorious slept, unconscious of his chains.
Round his large limbs were wound a thousand strings
By the weak hands of Confessors and Kings;
O'er his closed eyes a triple veil was bound,
And steely rivets lock'd him to the ground;
While stern Bastille with iron cage inthralls
His folded limbs, and hems in marble walls.
Touch'd by the patriot-flame, he rent amazed
The flimsy bonds, and round and round him gazed;
Starts up from earth, above the admiring throng
Lifts his colossal form, and towers along.
High o'er his foes his hundred arms he rears:
Plowshares his swords, and pruning-hooks his spears;
Calls to the Good and Brave with voice that rolls
Like Heaven's own thunder round the echoing Poles;
Gives to the winds his banner broad unfurl'd,
And gathers in its shade the living world!

VII " Gnomes! you then taught volcanic airs to force
Through bubbling lavas their resistless course,
O'er the broad walls of rifted granite climb,
And pierce the rent roof of incumbent lime;

---

25 wanting feathers, bare [JD]

Round sparry caves metallic lustres fling,
And bear phlogiston[26] on their tepid wing.

" Hence glow, refulgent tin! thy crystal grains,
And tawny copper shoots her azure veins;
Zinc lines his fretted vault with sable ore,
And dull galena tessellates the floor.
On vermil beds in Idria's mighty caves
The living silver rolls its ponderous waves;
With gay refractions bright platina shines,
And studs with squander'd[27] stars his dusky mines.
Long threads of netted gold, and silvery darts,
Inlay the lazuli and pierce the quartz.
Whence roof'd with silver beam'd Peru, of old,
And hapless Mexico was paved with gold.

" Heavens! on my sight what sanguine colours blaze!
Spain's deathless shame! the crimes of modern days!
When Avarice, shrouded in Religion's robe
Sail'd to the west and slaughter'd half the globe;
While Superstition, stalking by his side,
Mock'd the loud groans and lapp'd the bloody tide;
For sacred truths announced her frenzied dreams,
And turn'd to night the sun's meridian beams.

" Hear, oh, Britannia! potent Queen of isles,
On whom fair Art and meek Religion smiles,
How Afric's coasts thy craftier sons invade
With murder, rapine, theft - and call it Trade!
The slave, in chains, on supplicating knee
Spreads his wide arms and lifts his eyes to thee,
With hunger pale, with wounds and toil oppress'd,
'Are we not brethren?' Sorrow chokes the rest.
Air! bear to heaven upon thy azure flood
Their innocent cries! - Earth! cover not their blood!

VIII " When Heaven's dread justice smites, in crimes o'ergrown,
The blood-nursed Tyrant on his purple throne,
Gnomes! your bold forms unnumber'd arms outstretch,
And urge the vengeance o'er the guilty wretch.
Thus when Cambyses led his barbarous hosts
From Persia's rocks to Egypt's trembling coasts,

---

[26] chemical liquor, very inflammable [JD]
[27] scattered [JD]

**Defiled each hallow'd fane and sacred wood,
And, drunk with fury, swell'd the Nile with blood;
Waved his proud banner o'er the Theban states,
And pour'd destruction through her hundred gates;
In dread divisions march'd the marshall'd bands,
And swarming armies blacken'd all the lands:
By Memphis these to Ethiop's sultry plains,
And those to Hammon's sand-incircled fanes.
Slow as they pass'd, the indignant Temples frown'd,
Low curses muttering from the vaulted ground;
Long aisles of cypress waved their deepen'd glooms,
And quivering spectres grinn'd amid the tombs;
Prophetic whispers breathed from Sphinx's tongue,
And Memnon's lyre with hollow murmurs rung;
Burst from each pyramid expiring groans,
And darker shadows stretch'd their lengthen'd cones.
Day after day their deathful rout they steer,
Lust in the van, and rapine in the rear.**

**" Gnomes! as they march'd you hid the gather'd fruits,
The bladed grass, sweet grains, and mealy roots;
Scared the tired quails that journey'd o'er their heads;
Retain'd the locusts in their earthy beds;
Bade on your sands no night-born dews distil;
Stay'd with vindictive hands the scanty rill.
Loud o'er the camp the Fiend of Famine shrieks,
Calls all her brood, and champs her hundred beaks;
O'er ten square leagues her pennons broad expand,
And twilight swims upon the shuddering sand;
Perch'd on her crest the Griffin Discord clings,
And Giant Murder rides between her wings:
Blood from each clotted hair and horny quill,
And showers of tears, in blended streams distil;
High poised in air her spiry neck she bends,
Rolls her keen eye, her dragon-claws extends,
Darts from above, and tears at each fell swoop
With iron fangs the decimated troop.**

**" Now o'er their head the whizzing whirlwinds breathe,
And the live desert pants and heaves beneath;
Tinged by the crimson sun, vast columns rise
Of eddying sands, and war amid the skies;
In red arcades the billowy plain surround,
And whirling turrets stalk along the ground.
Long ranks in vain their shining blades extend,
To demon-gods their knees unhallow'd bend,**

Wheel in wide circle, form in hollow square,
And now they front, and now they fly the war,
Pierce the deaf tempest with lamenting cries,
Press their parch'd lips and close their blood-shot eyes.

" Gnomes! o'er the waste you led your myriad powers,
Climb'd on the whirls and aim'd the flinty showers!
Onward resistless rolls the infuriate surge,
Clouds follow clouds, and mountains mountains urge;
Wave over wave the driving desert swims,
Bursts o'er their heads, inhumes their struggling limbs.
Man mounts on man, on camels camels rush,
Hosts march o'er hosts, and nations nations crush.
Wheeling in air the winged islands fall
And one great earthy ocean covers all!
Then ceased the storm. Night bow'd his Ethiop brow
To earth and listen'd to the groans below.
Grim Horror shook; awhile the living hill
Heaved with convulsive throes; and all was still!

IX " Gnomes! whose fine forms, impassive as the air,
Shrink with soft sympathy for human care;
Who glide unseen, on printless slippers borne,
Beneath the waving grass and nodding corn;
Or lay your tiny limbs, when noon-tide warms,
Where shadowy cowslips stretch their golden arms.
So, marked on orreries in lucid signs,
Starr'd with bright points, the mimic zodiac shines;
Borne on fine wires amid the pictured skies
With ivory orbs the planets set and rise;
Round the dwarf Earth the pearly Moon is roll'd,
And the Sun twinkling whirls his rays of gold.
Call your bright myriads, march your mailed hosts,
With spears and helmets, glittering round the coasts:
Thick as the hairs which rear the lion's mane,
Or fringe the boar that bays the hunter-train.

" Watch! where proud surges break their treacherous mounds
And sweep resistless o'er the cultur'd grounds.
Such as erewhile, impell'd o'er Belgia's plain,
Roll'd her rich ruins to the insatiate main.
With piles and piers the ruffian waves engage,
And bid indignant Ocean stay his rage.
Where girt with clouds the rifted mountain yawns,
And chills with length of shade the gelid lawns,

Climb the rude steeps, the granite-cliffs surround,
Pierce with steel points, with wooden wedges wound;
Break into clays the soft volcanic slags,
Or melt with acid airs the marble crags;
Crown the green summits with adventurous flocks,
And charm with novel flowers the wondering rocks.
So when proud Rome the Afric Warrior braved,
And high on Alps his crimson banner waved,
While rocks on rocks their beetling brows oppose
With piny forests and unfathom'd snows,
Onward he march'd to Latium's velvet ground,
With fires and acids burst the obdurate bound;
Wide o'er her weeping vales destruction hurl'd, [28]
And shook the rising empire of the world.

X " Go, gentle Gnomes! resume your vernal toil,
Seek my chill tribes which sleep beneath the soil;
On grey-moss banks, green meads, or furrow'd lands
Spread the dark mould, white lime, and crumbling sands;
Each bursting bud with healthier juices feed:
Emerging scion or awakened seed.
So in descending streams the silver chyle[29]
Streaks with white clouds the golden floods of bile;
Through each nice valve the mingling currents glide,
Join their fine rills, and swell the sanguine tide;
Each countless cell and viewless fibre seek,
Nerve the strong arm and tinge the blushing cheek.
Oh, watch where, bosom'd in the teeming earth,
Green swells the germ, impatient for its birth;
Guard from rapacious worms its tender shoots,
And drive the mining beetle from its roots;
With ceaseless efforts rend the obdurate clay,
And give my vegetable babes to day!
Thus when an Angel-form, in light array'd,
Like Howard pierced the prison's noisome shade,
Where chain'd to earth, with eyes to heaven upturn'd,
The kneeling saint in holy anguish mourn'd;
Ray'd from his lucid vest and halo'd brow
O'er the dark roof celestial lustres glow.
'Peter, arise!' with cheering voice he calls,
And sounds seraphic echo round the walls;

---

[28] The first editor miscalculates by 5 lines here, as again between lines 545 and 555. [ed.]
[29] white juice of the stomach [JD]

Locks, bolts and chains his potent touch obey,
And pleased he leads the dazzled sage to day.

XI “ You! whose fine fingers fill the organic cells
With virgin earth, of woods and bones and shells;
Mould with retractile glue their spongy beds,
And stretch and strengthen all their fibre-threads.
Late when the mass obeys its changeful doom
And sinks to earth, its cradle and its tomb,
Gnomes! with nice eye the slow solution watch,
With fostering hand the parting atoms catch,
Join in new forms, combine with life and sense,
And guide and guard the transmigrating Ens.

“ So when on Lebanon’s sequester’d height
The fair Adonis left the realms of light,
Bow’d his bright locks and, fated from his birth
To change eternal, mingled with the earth.
With darker horror shook the conscious wood,
Groan’d the sad gales, and rivers blush’d with blood;
On cypress-boughs the Loves their quivers hung,
Their arrows scatter’d and their bows unstrung,
And Beauty’s goddess, bending o’er his bier,
Breath’d the soft sigh and pour’d the tender tear.
Admiring Proserpine through dusky glades
Led the fair phantom to Elysian shades,
Clad with new form, with finer sense combined,
And lit with purer flame the ethereal mind.
Erewhile, emerging from infernal night,
The bright assurgent rises into light,
Leaves the drear chambers of the insatiate tomb,
And shines and charms with renovated bloom.
While wondering Loves the bursting grave surround,
And edge with meeting wings the yawning ground;
Stretch their fair necks and, leaning o’er the brink,
View the pale regions of the dead, and shrink.
Long with broad eyes ecstatic Beauty stands,
Heaves her white bosom, spreads her waxen hands;
Then with loud shriek the panting youth alarms:
‘My life! my love!’ and springs into his arms.”

The Goddess ceased. The delegated throng
O’er the wide plains delighted rush along;
In dusky squadrons and in shining groups,
Hosts follow hosts, and troops succeed to troops.

**Scarce bears the bending grass the moving freight,
And nodding florets bow beneath their weight.
So when light clouds on airy pinions sail,
Flit the soft shadows o'er the waving vale;
Shade follows shade, as laughing Zephyrs drive,
And all the chequer'd landscape seems alive.**

End of Canto Two

Canto Three

(The Element of Water)

Again the Goddess speaks! Glad Echo swells
The tuneful tones along her shadowy dells,
Her wrinkling founts with soft vibration shakes,
Curls her deep wells and rimples all her lakes;
Thrills each wide stream Britannia's isle that laves,
Her headlong cataracts and circumfluent waves.
Thick as the dews which deck the morning flowers,
Or rain-drops twinkling in the sun-bright showers,
Fair Nymphs, emerging in pellucid bands,
Rise as she turns, and whiten all the lands.

I " Your buoyant troops on dimpling ocean tread,
Wafting the moist air from his oozy bed,
Aquatic Nymphs! you lead with viewless march
The winged vapours up the aerial arch;
On each broad cloud a thousand sails expand,
And steer the shadowy treasure o'er the land;
Through vernal skies the gathering drops diffuse,
Plunge in soft rains, or sink in silver dews.
Your lucid bands condense with fingers chill
The blue mist hovering round the gelid hill;
In clay-form'd beds the trickling streams collect,
Strain through white sands, through pebbly veins direct,
Or point in rifted rocks their dubious way,
And in each bubbling fountain rise to day.

" Nymphs! you then guide, attendant from their source,
The associate rills along their sinuous course;
Float in bright squadrons by the willowy brink,
Or circling slow in limpid eddies sink;
Call from her crystal cave the Naiad-Nymph
And, as below she braids her hyaline[30] hair,
Eyes her soft smiles reflected in the air;
Or sport in groups with river-boys, that lave
Their silken limbs amid the dashing wave;
Pluck the pale primrose bending from its edge,
Or, tittering, dance amid the whispering sedge.

---

[30] i.e. transparent like glass [ed.]

" Onward you pass, the pine-capt hills divide,
Or feed the golden harvests on their side;
The wide-ribb'd arch with hurrying torrents fill,
Shove the slow barge, or whirl the foaming mill;
Or lead with beckoning hand the sparkling train
Of refluent water to its parent main,
And, pleased, revisit in their sea-moss vales
Blue Nereid-forms array'd in shining scales;
Shapes, whose broad oar the torpid wave impels,
And Tritons bellowing through their twisted shells.

" So from the heart the sanguine stream distils
O'er Beauty's radiant shrine in vermil rills,
Feeds each fine nerve, each slender hair pervades,
The skin's bright snow with living purple shades,
Each dimpling cheek with warmer blushes dyes,
Laughs on the lips, and lightens in the eyes.
Erewhile absorb'd, the vagrant globules swim
From each fair feature and proportion'd limb,
Join'd in one trunk with deeper tint return
To the warm concave of the vital urn.

II.i " Aquatic Maids! you sway the mighty realms
Of scale and shell, which Ocean overwhelms;
As Night's pale Queen her rising orb reveals,
And climbs the zenith with refulgent wheels,
Car'd on the foam your glimmering legion rides;
Your little tridents heave the dashing tides,
Urge on the sounding shores their crystal course,
Restrain their fury, or direct their force.

ii " Nymphs! you adorn, in glossy volutes[31] roll'd,
The gaudy conch with azure, green, and gold.
You round Echinus ray his arrowy mail,
Give the keel'd Nautilus his oar and sail;
Firm to his rock with silver cords suspend
The anchor'd Pinna and his Cancer-friend;
With worm-like beard his toothless lips array,
And teach the unwieldy Sturgeon to betray:
Ambush'd in weeds, or sepulchred in sands,
In dread repose he waits the scaly bands,
Waves in red spires the living lures, and draws
The unwary plunderers to his circling jaws,

31 convolutions [ed.]

Eyes with grim joy the twinkling shoals beset
And clasps the quick inextricable net.
You chase the warrior Shark and cumbrous Whale,
And guard the Mermaid in her briny vale;
Feed the live petals of her insect-flowers,
Her shell-wrack gardens, and her sea-fan bowers;
With ores and gems adorn her coral cell,
And drop a pearl in every gaping shell.

iii " Your myriad trains o'er stagnant oceans tow
(Harness'd with gossamer) the loitering prow;
Or, with fine films (suspended o'er the deep)
Of oil effusive, lull the waves to sleep.
You stay the flying bark, conceal'd beneath,
Where living rocks of worm-built coral breathe;
Meet fell Teredo, as he mines the keel
With beaked head, and break his lips of steel;
Turn the broad helm, the fluttering canvas urge,
From Maelstrom's fierce innavigable surge.
'Mid the lorn isles of Norway's stormy main,
As sweeps o'er many a league his eddying train,
Vast watery walls in rapid circles spin,
And deep-ingulph'd the Demon dwells within;
Springs o'er the fear-froze crew with Harpy-claws;
Down his deep den the whirling vessel draws;
Churns with his bloody mouth the dread repast,
The booming waters murmuring o'er the mast.

III " Where with chill frown enormous Alps alarms
A thousand realms, horizon'd in his arms;
While cloudless suns meridian glories shed
From skies of silver round his hoary head,
Tall rocks of ice refract the coloured rays,
And Frost sits throned amid the lambent blaze;
Nymphs! your thin forms pervade his glittering piles,
His roofs of crystal, and his glassy aisles;
Where in cold caves imprison'd Naiads sleep,
Or chain'd on mossy couches wake and weep;
Where round dark crags indignant waters bend
Through rifted ice, in ivory veins descend,
Seek through unfathom'd snows their devious track,
Heave the vast spars, the ribbed granites crack,
Rush into day, in foamy torrents shine,
And swell the imperial Danube or the Rhine.
Or feed the murmuring Tiber, as he laves
His realms inglorious with diminish'd waves;

Hears his lorn Forum sound with eunuch-strains,
Sees dancing slaves insult his martial plains;
Parts with chill stream the dim religious bower,
Time-moulder'd bastion and dismantled tower;
By alter'd fanes and nameless villas glides,
And classic domes, that tremble on his sides;
Sighs o'er each broken urn and yawning tomb,
And mourns the fall of Liberty and Rome.

IV " Sailing in air, when dark Monsoon inshrouds
His tropic mountains in a night of clouds;
Or drawn by whirlwinds from the Line returns,
And showers o'er Afric all his thousand urns;
High o'er his head the beams of Sirius glow,
And, dog of Nile, Anubis barks below.
Nymphs! you from cliff to cliff attendant guide
In headlong cataracts the impetuous tide;
Or lead, o'er wastes of Abyssinian sands,
The bright expanse to Egypt's shower-less lands.
Her long canals the sacred waters fill,
And edge with silver every peopled hill;
Gigantic Sphinx in circling waves admire,
And Memnon bending o'er his broken lyre;
O'er furrow'd glebes and green savannas sweep,
And towns and temples laugh amid the deep.

V. i " High in the frozen north where Heccla glows,
And melts in torrents his coeval snows,
O'er isles and oceans sheds a sanguine light,
Or shoots red stars amid the ebon night;
When, at his base intomb'd, with bellowing sound
Fell Geyser roar'd, and struggling shook the ground;
Pour'd from red nostrils, with her scalding breath,
A boiling deluge o'er the blasted heath;
And, wide in air, in misty volumes hurl'd
Contagious atoms o'er the alarmed world;
Nymphs! your bold myriads broke the infernal spell,
And crushed the Sorceress in her flinty cell.

ii " Where with soft fires in unextinguish'd urns,
Cauldron'd in rock, innocuous lava burns,
On the bright lake your gelid hands distil
In pearly showers the parsimonious rill;
And, as aloft the curling vapours rise
Through the cleft roof, ambitious for the skies,

In vaulted hills condense the tepid steams,
And pour to Health the medicated streams.
So in green vales amid her mountains bleak
Buxtonia smiles, the Goddess-Nymph of Peak;
Deep in warm waves and pebbly baths she dwells,
And calls Hygeia to her sainted wells.

" Hither in sportive bands bright Devon leads
Graces and Loves from Chatsworth's flowery meads.
Charm'd round the Nymph, they climb the rifted rocks,
And steep in mountain-mist their golden locks;
On venturous step her sparry caves explore,
And light with radiant eyes her realms of ore.
Oft by her bubbling founts and shadowy domes,
In gay undress the fairy legion roams;
Their dripping palms in playful malice fill,
Or taste with ruby lip the sparkling rill;
Crowd round her baths, and, bending o'er the side,
Unclasp'd their sandals, and their zones untied,
Dip with gay fear the shuddering foot undress'd,
And quick retract it to the fringed vest;
Or cleave with brandish'd arms the lucid stream,
And sob, their blue eyes twinkling in the steam.
High o'er the chequer'd vault with transient glow
Bright lustres dart, as dash the waves below;
And Echo's sweet responsive voice prolongs
The dulcet tumult of their silver tongues.
O'er their flush'd cheeks uncurling tresses flow,
And dew-drops glitter on their necks of snow;
Round each fair Nymph her dropping mantle clings,
And Loves emerging shake their showery wings.

" Here oft her Lord surveys the rude domain,
Fair arts of Greece triumphant in his train.
Lo! as he steps, the column'd pile ascends,
The blue roof closes, or the crescent bends;
New woods aspiring clothe their hills with green,
Smooth slope the lawns, the grey rock peeps between;
Relenting Nature gives her hand to Taste,
And Health and Beauty crown the laughing waste.

VI " Nymphs! your bright squadrons watch with chemic eyes
The cold elastic[32] vapours as they rise;

[32] i.e. expanding [ed.]

**With playful force arrest them as they pass,
And to pure Air betroth the flaming Gas[33].
Round their translucent forms at once they fling
Their rapturous arms, with silver bosoms cling;
In fleecy clouds their fluttering wings extend,
Or from the skies in lucid showers descend;
Whence rills and rivers owe their secret birth,
And Ocean's hundred arms infold the earth.**

**" So, robed by Beauty's Queen, with softer charms
Saturnia woo'd the Thunderer to her arms;
O'er her fair limbs a veil of light she spread,
And bound a starry diadem on her head;
Long braids of pearl her golden tresses graced,
And the charm'd Cestus sparkled round her waist.
Raised o'er the woof, by Beauty's hand inwrought,
Breathes the soft sigh, and glows the enamour'd thought.
Vows on light wings succeed, and quiver'd wiles,
Assuasive accents and seductive smiles.
Slow rolls the Cyprian car in purple pride
And, steer'd by Love, ascends admiring Ide;
Climbs the green slopes, the nodding woods pervades,
Burns round the rocks, or gleams amid the shades.
Glad Zephyr leads the train and waves above
The barbed darts and blazing torch of Love;
Reverts his smiling face and, pausing, flings
Soft showers of roses from aurelian[34] wings.
Delighted Fawns, in wreaths of flowers array'd,
With tiptoe wood-boys beat the chequer'd glade.
Alarmed Naiads, rising into air,
Lift o'er their silver urns their leafy hair;
Each to her oak the bashful Dryads shrink,
And azure eyes are seen through every chink.
Love culls a flaming shaft of broadest wing
And rests the fork upon the quivering string;
Points his arch eye aloft, with fingers strong
Draws to his curled ear the silken thong;
Loud twangs the steel, the golden arrow flies,
Trails a long line of lustre through the skies.
' 'Tis done!' he shouts, 'the mighty Monarch feels!'
And with loud laughter shakes the silver wheels;**

---

[33] i.e. combine oxygen and hydrogen [ed.]
[34] i.e. butterfly [ed.]

Bends o'er the car and whirling, as it moves,
His loosen'd bowstring, drives the rising doves.
Pierced on his throne the starting Thunderer turns,
Melts with soft sighs, with kindling rapture burns;
Clasps her fair hand, and eyes in fond amaze
The bright intruder with enamour'd gaze.
'And leaves my Goddess, like a blooming bride,
The fanes of Argos for the rocks of Ide?
Her gorgeous palaces and amaranth[35] bowers
For cliff-topp'd mountains and aerial towers?'
He said; and, leading from her ivory seat
The blushing Beauty to his lone retreat,
Curtain'd with night the couch imperial shrouds,
And rests the crimson cushions upon clouds.
Earth feels the grateful influence from above,
Sighs the soft Air, and Ocean murmurs love;
Ethereal Warmth expands his brooding wing,
And in still showers descends the genial Spring.

VII " Nymphs of aquatic Taste! whose placid smile
Breathes sweet enchantment o'er Britannia's isle;
Whose sportive touch in showers resplendent flings
Her lucid cataracts and her bubbling springs;
Through peopled vales the liquid silver guides,
And swells in bright expanse her freighted tides.
You with nice ear, in tiptoe trains, pervade
Dim walks of morn or evening's silent shade;
Join the lone nightingale her woods among,
And roll your rills symphonious to her song;
Through fount-full dells and wave-worn valleys move,
And tune their echoing waterfalls to love;
Or catch, attentive to the distant roar,
The pausing murmurs of the dashing shore;
Or, as aloud she pours her liquid strain,
Pursue the Nereid on the twilight main.
Her playful sea-horse woos her soft commands,
Turns his quick ears, his webbed claws expands;
His watery way with waving volutes wins,
Or listening librates[36] on unmoving fins.
The Nymph emerging mounts her scaly seat,
Hangs o'er his glossy sides her silver feet,

---

35 containing flowers that never fade, i.e. immortal [ed.]
36 balances [JD]

With snow-white hands her arching veil detains,
Gives to his slimy lips the slacken'd reins,
Lifts to the star of eve her eye serene,
And chaunts the birth of Beauty's radiant Queen.
O'er her fair brow her pearly comb unfurls
Her beryl locks, and parts the waving curls;
Each tangled braid with glistening teeth unbinds
And with the floating treasure musks the winds.
Thrill'd by the dulcet accents, as she sings,
The rippling wave in widening circles rings;
Night's shadowy forms along the margin gleam
With pointed ears, or dance upon the stream;
The Moon transported stays her bright career,
And maddening stars shoot headlong from the sphere.

VIII " Nymphs! whose fair eyes with vivid lustres glow
For human weal, and melt at human woe,
Late as you floated on your silver shells
Sorrowing and slow by Derwent's willowy dells,
Where by tall groves his foamy flood he steers
Through ponderous arches, o'er impetuous weirs,
By Derby's shadowy towers reflective sweeps,
And gothic grandeur chills his dusky deeps,
You pearl'd with Pity's drops his velvet sides,
Sigh'd in his gales, and murmur'd in his tides,
Waved o'er his fringed brink a deeper gloom,
And bow'd his alders o'er Milcena's tomb.

" Oft with sweet voice she led her infant-train,
Printing with graceful step his spangled plain,
Explored his twinkling swarms that swim or fly,
And mark'd his florets with botanic eye.
'Sweet bud of Spring! how frail thy transient bloom;
Fine film,' she cried, ' of Nature's fairest loom!
Soon Beauty fades upon its damask throne!'
(Unconscious of the worm that mined her own!)
Pale are those lips where soft caresses hung,
Wan the warm cheek and mute the tender tongue;
Cold rests that feeling heart on Derwent's shore,
And those love-lighted eye-balls roll no more!
[Here her sad consort, stealing through the gloom (i)[37]
Of murmuring cloisters, gazes on her tomb;

---

[37] These twenty lines are inserted in the 1824 edition. [ed.]

Hangs in mute anguish o'er the scutcheon'd hearse,
Or graves with trembling style the votive verse:

'Sexton! oh, lay beneath this sacred shrine,
When Time's cold hand shall close my aching eyes,
Oh, gently lay this wearied earth of mine
Where wrapp'd in night my loved Milcena lies.

So shall with purer joy my spirit move
When the last trumpet thrills the caves of Death;
Catch the first whispers of my waking love
And drink with holy kiss her kindling breath.

The spotless Fair, with blush ethereal warm,
Shall hail with sweeter smile returning day;
Rise from her marble bed a brighter form
And win on buoyant step her airy way.

Shall bend approved, where beckoning hosts invite
On clouds of silver, her adoring knee;
Approach with Seraphim the throne of light,
And Beauty plead with angel-tongue for me!']

IX " Your virgin trains on Brindley's cradle smiled,
And nursed with fairy-love the unletter'd child,
Spread round his pillow all your sacred spells,
Pierced all your springs, and open'd all your wells.
As now on grass, with glossy folds reveal'd,
Glides the bright serpent, now in flowers conceal'd;
Far shine the scales that gild his sinuous back,
And lucid undulations mark his track;
So with strong arm immortal Brindley leads
His long canals, and parts the velvet meads;
Winding in lucid lines, the watery mass
Mines the firm rock, or loads the deep morass,
With rising locks a thousand hills alarms,
Flings o'er a thousand streams its silver arms,
Feeds the long vale, the nodding woodland laves,
And Plenty, Arts, and Commerce freight the waves.
Nymphs! who erewhile round Brindley's early bier
On snow-white bosoms shower'd the incessant tear,
Adorn his tomb! oh, raise the marble bust,
Proclaim his honours, and protect his dust!
With urns inverted round the sacred shrine
Their ozier wreaths let weeping Naiads twine;

While on the top Mechanic Genius stands,
Counts the fleet waves, and balances the lands.

X “ Nymphs! you first taught to pierce the caves
Of humid earth and lift her ponderous waves;
Bade with quick stroke the sliding piston bear
The viewless columns of incumbent air:
Press’d by the incumbent air, the floods below
Through opening valves in foaming torrents flow,
Foot after foot with lessen’d impulse move,
And rising seek the vacancy[38] above.
So when the mother, bending o’er his charms,
Clasps her fair nursling in delighted arms,
Throws the thin kerchief from her neck of snow,
And half unveils the pearly orbs below,
With sparkling eyes the blameless plunderer owns
Her soft embraces and endearing tones,
Seeks the salubrious fount with opening lips,
Spreads his inquiring hands, and smiles, and sips.

“ Connubial Fair! whom no fond transport warms
To lull your infant in maternal arms;
Who, bless’d in vain with tumid bosoms, hear
His tender wailings with unfeeling ear;
The soothing kiss and milky rill deny
To the sweet parting lip and glistening eye!
Ah! what avails the cradle’s damask roof,
The eider bolster, and embroider’d woof!
Oft hears the gilded couch unpitied plains[39],
And many a tear the tassell’d cushion stains!
No voice so sweet attunes his cares to rest,
So soft no pillow as his mother’s breast!
Thus charm’d to sweet repose, when twilight hours
Shed their soft influence on celestial bowers,
The cherub Innocence, with smile divine,
Shuts his white wings and sleeps on Beauty’s shrine.

XI “ From dome to dome when flames infuriate climb,
Sweep the long street, invest the tower sublime;
Gild the tall vanes amid the astonish’d night,
And reddening heaven returns the sanguine light;

[38] i.e. vacuum [ed.]
[39] i.e. complaints [ed.]

While with vast strides and bristling hair aloof
Pale Danger glides along the falling roof,
And Giant Terror howling in amaze
Moves his dark limbs across the lurid blaze,
Nymphs! you first taught the gelid wave to rise,
Hurl'd in resplendent arches to the skies;
In iron cells condensed the airy spring,
And imp'd the torrent with unfailing wing.
On the fierce flames the shower impetuous falls,
And sudden darkness shrouds the shatter'd walls;
Steam, smoke, and dust in blended volumes roll,
And Night and Silence repossess the Pole.

" Where were ye, Nymphs! in those disastrous hours
Which wrapp'd in flames Augusta's sinking towers?
Why did ye linger in your wells and groves
When sad Woodmason mourn'd her infant loves?
When thy fair daughters with unheeded screams,
Ill-fated Molesworth! [40] **call'd the loitering streams?**
The trembling nymph, on bloodless fingers hung,
Eyes from the tottering wall the distant throng,
With ceaseless shrieks her sleeping friends alarms,
Drops with singed hair into her lover's arms.
The illumin'd mother seeks, with footsteps fleet,
Where hangs the safe balcony o'er the street;
Wrapp'd in her sheet her youngest hope suspends,
And panting lowers it to her tiptoe friends;
Again she hurries on affection's wings,
And now a third, and now a fourth, she brings;
Safe all her babes, she smooths her horrent brow
And bursts through bickering flames, unscorch'd, below.
So, by her son arraign'd, with feet unshod
O'er burning bars indignant Emma trod.

" E'en on the day when Youth with Beauty wed,
The flames surprised them in their nuptial bed;
Seen at the opening sash with bosom bare,
With wringing hands and dark dishevell'd hair,
The blushing Beauty, with disorder'd charms,
Round her fond lover winds her ivory arms;
Beat, as they clasp, their throbbing hearts with fear;
And many a kiss is mixed with many a tear.

[40] reported in *The Gentleman's Magazine*, Vol. XXXIII (1763), p.255 [ed.]

Ah me! in vain the labouring engines pour
Round their pale limbs the ineffectual shower!
Then crash'd the floor, while shrinking crowds retire,
And Love and Virtue sunk amid the fire!
With piercing screams afflicted strangers mourn,
And their white ashes mingle in their urn.

XII "Pellucid forms! whose crystal bosoms show
The shine of welfare, or the shade of woe;
Who with soft lips salute returning Spring,
And hail the Zephyr quivering on his wing;
Or watch, untired, the wintry clouds, and share
With streaming eyes my vegetable care;
Go, shove the dim mist from the mountain's brow,
Chase the white fog which floods the vale below;
Melt the thick snows that linger on the lands,
And catch the hailstones in your little hands;
Guard the coy blossom from the pelting shower,
And dash the rimy spangles from the bower:
From each chill leaf the silvery drops repel,
And close the timorous floret's golden bell.

"So should young Sympathy, in female form,
Climb the tall rock, spectatress of the storm;
Life's sinking wrecks with secret sighs deplore,
And bleed for other's woes, herself on shore;
To friendless Virtue, gasping on the strand,
Bare her warm heart, her virgin arms expand;
Charm with kind looks, with tender accents cheer,
And pour the sweet consolatory tear;
Grief's cureless wounds with lenient balms assuage,
Or prop with firmer staff the steps of Age;
The lifted arm of mute Despair arrest,
And snatch the dagger pointed to his breast;
Or lull to slumber Envy's haggard mien,
And rob her quiver'd shafts with hand unseen.
Sound, Nymphs of Helicon! the trump of Fame,
And teach Hibernian echoes Jones's name;
Bind round her polish'd brow the civic bay,
And drag the fair philanthropist to day.
So from secluded springs and secret caves
Her Liffey pours his bright meandering waves,
Cools the parch'd vale, the sultry mead divides,
And towns and temples star his shadowy sides.

XIII “ Call your light legions, tread the swampy heath,
Pierce with sharp spades the tremulous peat beneath;
With coulters bright the rushy sward bisect,
And in new veins the gushing rills direct.
So flowers shall rise in purple light array’d,
And blossom’d orchards stretch their silver shade;
Admiring glebes their amber ears unfold,
And Labour sleep amid the waving gold.

“ Thus when young Hercules with firm disdain
Braved the soft smiles of Pleasure’s harlot train,
To valiant toils his forceful limbs assign’d,
And gave to Virtue all his mighty mind.
Fierce Achelous rush’d from mountain-caves,
O’er sad Etolia pour’d his wasteful waves,
O’er lowing vales and bleating pastures roll’d,
Swept her red vineyards and her glebes of gold;
Mined all her towns, uptore her rooted woods,
And Famine danced upon the shining floods.
The youthful Hero seized his curled crest,
And dash’d with lifted club the watery Pest;
With waving arm the billowy tumult quell’d,
And to his course the bellowing Fiend repell’d.
Then to a snake the finny Demon turn’d
His lengthen’d form, with scales of silver burn’d;
Lash’d with resistless sweep his dragon-train
And shot meandering o’er the affrighted plain.
The Hero-God, with giant fingers clasp’d
Firm round his neck, the hissing monster grasp’d;
With starting eyes, wide throat, and gaping teeth,
Curl his redundant folds and writhe in death.

“ And now a bull, amid the flying throng
The grisly Demon foam’d and roar’d along;
With silver hoofs the flowery meadow spurn’d,
Roll’d his red eye, his threatening antlers turn’d.
Dragg’d down to earth, the Warrior’s victor-hands
Press’d his deep dewlap on the imprinted sands;
Then with quick bound his bended knee he fix’d
High on his neck, the branching horns betwixt,
Strain’d his strong arms, his sinewy shoulders bent,
And from his curled brow the twisted terror rent.
Pleased Fawns and Nymphs with dancing step applaud
And hang their chaplets round the resting god;
Link their soft hands, and rear with pausing toil
The golden trophy on the furrow’d soil;

Fill with ripe fruits, with wreathed flowers adorn,
And give to Plenty her prolific horn.

XIV " On Spring's fair lap, cerulean Sisters! pour
From airy urns the sun-illumined shower,
Feed with the dulcet drops my tender broods,
Mellifluous flowers and aromatic buds;
Hang from each bending grass and horrent thorn
The tremulous pearl that glitters to the morn;
Or where cold dews their secret channels lave,
And Earth's dark chambers hide the stagnant wave,
O, pierce, ye Nymphs! her marble veins, and lead
Her gushing fountains to the thirsty mead;
Wide o'er the shining vales and trickling hills
Spread the bright treasure in a thousand rills.
So shall my peopled realms of Leaf and Flower
Exult, inebriate with the genial shower;
Dip their long tresses from the mossy brink,
With tufted roots the glassy currents drink;
Shade your cool mansions from meridian beams,
And view their waving honours in your streams.

" Thus where the veins their confluent branches bend,
And milky eddies with the purple blend,
The chyle's white trunk, diverging from its source,
Seeks through the vital mass its shining course;
O'er each red cell and tissued membrane spreads
In living net-work all its branching threads;
Maze within maze its tortuous path pursues,
Winds into glands, inextricable clews[41];
Steals through the stomach's velvet sides, and sips
The silver surges with a thousand lips;
Fills each fine pore, pervades each slender hair,
And drinks salubrious dew-drops from the air.

" Thus when to kneel in Mecca's awful gloom,
Or press with pious kiss Medina's tomb,
League after league through many a lingering day
Steer the swart caravans their sultry way;
O'er sandy wastes on gasping camels toil,
Or print with pilgrim-steps the burning soil;
If from lone rocks a sparkling rill descend,
O'er the green brink the kneeling nations bend,

---

41 i.e. threads [ed.]

Bathe the parch'd lip and cool the feverish tongue,
And the clear lake reflects the mingled throng."

The Goddess paused; the listening bands awhile
Still seem to hear and dwell upon her smile;
Then with soft murmur sweep in lucid trains
Down the green slopes and o'er the pebbly plains;
To each bright stream on silver sandals glide,
Reflective fountain, and tumultuous tide.

So shoot the spider-broods at breezy dawn
Their glittering net-work o'er the autumnal lawn;
From blade to blade connect with cordage fine
The unbending grass, and live along the line;
Or bathe unwet their oily forms, and dwell
With feet repulsive on the dimpling well.

So when the North congeals his watery mass,
Piles high his snows, and floors his seas with glass;
While many a month, unknown to warmer rays,
Marks its slow chronicle by lunar days;
Stout youths and ruddy damsels, sportive train,
Leave the white soil and rush upon the main;
From isle to isle the moon-bright squadrons stray,
And win in easy curves their graceful way;
On step alternate borne, with balance nice
Hang o'er the gliding steel, and hiss along the ice.

End of Canto Three

Canto Four

(The Element of Air)

As when at noon in Hybla's fragrant bowers
Cacalia opens all her honey'd flowers,
Contending swarms on bending branches cling,
And nations hover on aurelian wing;
So round the Goddess, ere she speaks, on high
Impatient Sylphs in gaudy circlets fly;
Quivering in air their painted plumes expand,
And colour'd shadows dance upon the land.

I " Sylphs! your light troops the tropic winds confine,
And guide their streaming arrows to the Line;
While in warm floods ecliptic breezes rise,
And sink with wings benumb'd in colder skies.
You bid monsoons on Indian seas reside,
And veer, as moves the sun, their airy tide;
While southern gales o'er western oceans roll,
And Eurus[42] steals his ice-winds from the Pole.
Your playful trains, on sultry islands born,
Turn on fantastic toe at eve and morn;
With soft susurrant voice alternate sweep
Earth's green pavilions and encircling deep;
Or in itinerant cohorts, borne sublime
On tides of ether, float from clime to clime;
O'er waving autumn bend your airy ring,
Or waft the fragrant bosom of the Spring.

II " When Morn, escorted by the dancing Hours,
O'er the bright plains her dewy lustre showers,
Till from her sable chariot Eve serene
Drops the dark curtain o'er the brilliant scene,
You form with chemic hands the airy surge,
Mix with broad vans[43], with shadowy tridents urge.
Sylphs! from each sun-bright leaf, that twinkling shakes
O'er earth's green lap or shoots amid her lakes,
Your playful bands with simpering lips invite,
And wed the enamour'd Oxygen to Light.
Round their white necks with fingers interwove,
Cling the fond pair with unabating love;

---

42 south-east wind [ed.]
43 wings [ed.]

Hand link'd in hand on buoyant step they rise,
And soar and glisten in unclouded skies.
Whence in bright floods the Vital Air expands,
And with concentric spheres involves the lands;
Pervades the swarming seas and heaving earths,
Where teeming nature broods her myriad births;
Fills the fine lungs of all that breathe or bud,
Warms the new heart and dyes the gushing blood;
With life's first spark inspires the organic frame
And, as it wastes, renews the subtle flame.

" So pure, so soft, with sweet attraction shone
Fair Psyche, kneeling at the ethereal throne;
Won with coy smiles the admiring court of Jove,
And warm'd the bosom of unconquer'd Love.
Beneath a moving shade of fruits and flowers
Onward they march to Hymen's sacred bowers;
With lifted torch he lights the festive train,
Sublime, and leads them in his golden chain;
Joins the fond pair, indulgent to their vows,
And hides with mystic veil their blushing brows.
Round their fair forms their mingling arms they fling,
Meet with warm lip and clasp with rustling wing.
Hence plastic Nature, as Oblivion whelms
Her fading forms, repeoples all her realms;
Soft Joys disport on purple plumes unfurl'd,
And Love and Beauty rule the willing world.

III. i " Sylphs! your bold myriads on the withering heath
Stay the fell Syroc's suffocative breath;
Arrest Simoom in his realms of sand,
The poison'd javelin balanced in his hand;
Fierce on blue streams he rides the tainted air,
Points his keen eye, and waves his whistling hair;
While, as he turns, the undulating soil
Rolls in red waves, and billowy deserts boil.
You seize Tornado by his locks of mist,
Burst his dense clouds, his wheeling spires untwist;
Wide o'er the west, when borne on headlong gales,
Dark as meridian night, the monster sails;
Howls high in air and shakes his curled brow,
Lashing with serpent-train the waves below;
Whirls his black arm, the forked lightning flings,
And showers a deluge from his demon-wings.

ii “ Sylphs! with light shafts you pierce the drowsy Fog
That lingering slumbers on the sedge-wove bog,
With webbed feet o’er midnight meadows creeps,
Or flings his hairy limbs on stagnant deeps.
You meet Contagion issuing from afar
And dash the baleful conqueror from his car,
When, guest of Death! from charnel vaults he steals,
And bathes in human gore his armed wheels.
Thus when the Plague, upborne on Belgian air,
Look’d through the mist and shook his clotted hair,
O’er shrinking nations steer’d malignant clouds,
And rain’d destruction on the gasping crowds,
The beauteous Aegle felt the venom’d dart,
Slow roll’d her eye and feebly throbb’d her heart;
Each fervid sigh seem’d shorter than the last,
And starting Friendship shunn’d her as she pass’d.
With weak unsteady step the fainting maid
Seeks the cold garden’s solitary shade,
Sinks on the pillowy moss her drooping head,
And prints with lifeless limbs her leafy bed.
On wings of love her plighted swain pursues,
Shades her from winds and shelters her from dews;
Extends on tapering poles the canvas roof;
Spreads o’er the straw-wove mat the flaxen woof;
Sweet buds and blossoms on her bolster strows,
And binds his kerchief round her aching brows;
Soothes with soft kiss, with tender accents charms,
And clasps the bright Infection in his arms.
With pale and languid smiles the grateful fair
Applauds his virtue, and rewards his care;
Mourns with wet cheek her fair companions, fled
On timorous step, or number’d with the dead;
Calls to her bosom all its scatter’d rays
And pours on Thyrsis the collected blaze;
Braves the chill night, caressing and caress’d,
And folds her hero-lover to her breast.
Less bold, Leander at the dusky hour
Eyed, as he swam, the far love-lighted tower;
Breasted with struggling arms the tossing wave,
And sunk benighted in the watery grave.
Less bold, Tobias claim’d the nuptial bed
Where seven fond lovers by a fiend had bled,
And drove, instructed by his angel-guide,
The enamour’d demon from the fatal bride.
Sylphs! while your winnowing pinions fann’d the air
And shed gay visions o’er the sleeping pair,

Love round their couch effused his rosy breath
And with his keener arrows conquer'd Death.

IV. i " You charm'd, indulgent Sylphs! their learned toil,
And crown'd with fame your Torricell and Boyle;
Taught with sweet smiles, responsive to their prayer,
The spring[44] and pressure of the viewless air:
How up exhausted tubes bright currents flow
Of liquid silver from the lake below,
Weigh the long column of the incumbent skies,
And with the changeful moment fall and rise.
How, as in brazen pumps the pistons move,
The membrane-valve sustains the weight above;
Stroke follows stroke, the gelid vapour falls,
And misty dew-drops dim the crystal walls;
Rare and more rare expands the fluid thin,
And silence dwells with vacancy within.
So in the mighty void, with grim delight,
Primeval Silence reign'd with ancient Night.

ii " Sylphs! your soft voices, whispering from the skies,
Bade from low earth the bold Montgolfier rise;
Outstretch'd his buoyant ball with airy spring,
And bore the sage on levity of wing.
Where were ye, Sylphs! when on the ethereal main
Young Rozier launch'd, and call'd your aid in vain?
Fair mounts the light balloon, by Zephyr driven,
Parts the thin clouds and sails along the heaven;
Higher and yet higher the expanding bubble flies,
Lights with quick flash, and bursts amid the skies.
Headlong he rushes through the affrighted air
With limbs distorted, and dishevell'd hair;
Whirls round and round, the flying crowd alarms,
And Death receives him in his sable arms!
[Betrothed beauty bending o'er his bier [45]
Breathes the loud sob and sheds the incessant tear;
Pursues the sad procession, as it moves
Through winding avenues and waving groves;
Hears the slow dirge amid the echoing aisles,
And mingles with her sighs discordant smiles.
Then with quick step advancing through the gloom,
'I come!' she cries, and leaps into his tomb.

---

44 elastic force [JD]
45 These twelve lines are inserted in the 1824 edition. [ed.]

'Oh, stay! I follow thee to realms above!
Oh, wait a moment for thy dying love! (x)
Thus, thus I clasp thee to my bursting heart!
Close o'er us, holy earth! We will not part!']

" So erst, with melting wax and loosen'd strings
Sunk hapless Icarus on unfaithful wings;
His scatter'd plumage danced upon the the wave,
And sorrowing mermaids deck'd his watery grave;
O'er his pale corse their pearly sea-flowers shed,
And strew'd with crimson moss his marble bed;
Struck in their coral towers the pausing bell,
And wide in ocean toll'd his echoing knell.

V " Sylphs! you, retiring to sequester'd bowers,
Where oft your Priestley woos your airy powers,
On noiseless step or quivering pinion glide,
As sits the sage with Science by his side;
To his charm'd eye in gay undress appear,
Or pour your secrets in his raptured ear:
How nitrous gas from iron ingots driven
Drinks with red lips the purest breath of heaven;
How, while Conferva from its tender hair
Gives in bright bubbles empyreal air[46],
The crystal floods[47] phlogistic ores calcine[48],
And the pure Ether marries with the Mine.

" So in Sicilia's ever-blooming shade
When playful Proserpine from Ceres stray'd,
Led with unwary step her virgin trains
O'er Etna's steeps, and Enna's golden plains;
Pluck'd with fair hand the silver-blossom'd bower
And purple mead - herself a fairer flower;
Sudden, unseen amid the twilight glade,
Rush'd gloomy Dis, and seized the trembling maid.
Her starting damsels sprung from mossy seats,
Dropp'd from their gauzy laps the gather'd sweets,
Clung round the struggling nymph, with piercing cries,
Pursued the chariot, and invoked the skies.
Pleased as he grasps her in his iron arms,
Frights with soft sighs, with tender words alarms.

---

[46] phrase used for oxygen by Scheele its co-discoverer. [ed.]
[47] i.e. colourless gas [ed.]
[48] apply heat, often leading to oxydation [ed.]

The wheels descending roll'd in smoky rings;
Infernal Cupids flapp'd their demon wings;
Earth with deep yawn received the Fair, amazed,
And far in night celestial beauty blazed.

VI "Led by the sage, Lo! Britain's sons shall guide
Huge sea-balloons beneath the tossing tide.
The diving castles, roof'd with spheric glass,
Ribb'd with strong oak, and barr'd with bolts of brass,
Buoy'd with pure air shall endless tracks pursue,
And Priestley's hand the vital flood renew.
Then shall Britannia rule the wealthy realms
Which ocean's wide insatiate wave o'erwhelms;
Confine in netted bowers his scaly flocks,
Part his blue plains, and people all his rocks.
Deep in warm waves beneath the Line that roll,
Beneath the shadowy ice-isles of the Pole,
Onward, through bright meandering vales afar,
Obedient sharks shall trail her sceptred car,
With harness'd necks the pearly flood disturb,
Stretch the silk rein, and champ the silver curb.
Pleased round her triumph wondering Tritons play,
And sea-maids hail her on the watery way.
Oft shall she weep beneath the crystal waves
O'er shipwreck'd lovers weltering in their graves;
Mingling in death the brave and good behold,
With slaves to glory, and with slaves to gold.
Shrined in the deep shall Day and Spalding mourn,
Each in his treacherous bell, sepulchral urn!
Oft o'er thy lovely daughters, hapless Pierce!
Her sighs shall breathe, her sorrows dew their hearse:
With brow upturn'd to heaven, 'We will not part!'
He cried, and clasp'd them to his aching heart.
Dash'd in dread conflict on the rocky grounds,
Crash'd the shock'd masts, the staggering wreck rebounds;
Through gaping seams the rushing deluge swims,
Chills their pale bosoms, bathes their shuddering limbs,
Climbs their white shoulders, buoys their streaming hair,
And the last sea-shriek bellows in the air.
Each with loud sobs her tender sire caress'd,
And gasping strain'd him closer to her breast!
Stretch'd on one bier they sleep beneath the brine,
And their white bones with ivory arms intwine!

VII "Sylphs of nice ear! with beating wings you guide
The fine vibrations of the aerial tide;

Join in sweet cadences the measured words,
Or stretch and modulate the trembling chords.
You strung to melody the Grecian lyre,
Breathed the rapt song and fann'd the thought of fire,
Or brought in combinations, deep and clear,
Immortal harmony to Handel's ear.
You with soft breath attune the vernal gale,
When breezy evening broods the listening vale;
Or wake the loud tumultuous sounds that dwell
In Echo's many-toned diurnal[49] shell.
You melt in dulcet chords when Zephyr rings
The Eolian Harp, and mingle all its strings;
Or trill in air the soft symphonious chime
When rapt Cecilia lifts her eye sublime;
Swell, as she breathes, her bosom's rising snow;
O'er her white teeth in tuneful accents flow;
Through her fair lips on whispering pinions move,
And form the tender sighs that kindle love!

" So playful Love on Ida's flowery sides
With ribbon-rein the indignant lion guides;
Pleased on his brinded back the lyre he rings,
And shakes delirious rapture from the strings.
Slow as the pausing monarch stalks along,
Sheaths his retractile claws and drinks the song.
Soft nymphs on timid step the triumph view,
And listening fawns with beating hoofs pursue.
With pointed ears the alarmed forest starts,
And love and music soften savage hearts.

VIII " Sylphs! your bold hosts, when Heaven with justice dread
Calls the red tempest round the guilty head,
Fierce at his nod assume vindictive forms,
And launch from airy cars the vollied storms.
From Ashur's vales when proud Sennacherib trod,
Pour'd his swoll'n heart, defied the living God,
Urged with incessant shouts his glittering powers,
And Judah shook through all her massy towers;
Round her sad altars press the prostrate crowd,
Hosts beat their breasts, and suppliant chieftains bow'd;
Loud shrieks of matrons thrill'd the troubled air,
And trembling virgins rent their scatter'd hair.

---

49 possibly 'two-urned' or 'bivalved' [ed.]

High in the midst the kneeling king adored,
Spread the blaspheming scroll before the Lord,
Raised his pale hands, and breathed his pausing sighs,
And fixed on heaven his dim imploring eyes:
'Oh! mighty God! amidst thy seraph-throng
Who sitt'st sublime, the judge of right and wrong;
Thine the wide Earth, bright Sun, and starry zone,
That twinkling journey round thy golden throne;
Thine the crystal source of life and light,
And thine the realms of death's eternal night.
Oh! bend thine ear, thy gracious eye incline,
Lo! Ashur's king blasphemes thy holy shrine,
Insults our offerings, and derides our vows.
Oh! strike the diadem from his impious brows,
Tear from from his murderous hand the bloody rod,
And teach the trembling nations "Thou art God!" '
Sylphs! in what dread array, with pennons broad,
Onward ye floated o'er the ethereal road;
Call'd each dank steam the reeking marsh exhales,
Contagious vapours, and volcanic gales;
Gave the soft South with poisonous breath to blow,
And roll'd the dreadful whirlwind on the foe!
Hark! o'er the camp the venom'd tempest sings,
Man falls on man, on buckler[50] buckler rings;
Groan answers groan, to anguish anguish yields,
And Death's loud accents shake the tented fields!
High rears the Fiend his grinning jaws, and wide
Spans the pale nations with colossal stride,
Waves his broad falchion with uplifted hand,
And his vast shadow darkens all the land.

IX. i " Ethereal cohorts! Essences of Air!
Make the green children of the Spring your care!
Oh, Sylphs! disclose in this inquiring age
One golden secret to some favour'd sage;
Grant the charm'd talisman: the chain that binds
Or guides the changeful pinions of the winds!
No more shall hoary Boreas, issuing forth
With Eurus, lead the tempests of the North;
Rime the pale Dawn, or veil'd in flaky showers
Chill the sweet bosoms of the smiling Hours.
By whispering Auster waked, shall Zephyr rise,
Meet with soft kiss and mingle in the skies,

---

[50] shield [ed.]

Fan the gay floret, bend the yellow ear,
And rock the uncurtain'd cradle of the year;
Autumn and Spring in lively union blend,
And from the skies the Golden Age descend.

ii "Castled on ice, beneath the circling Bear,
A vast chameleon spits and swallows air;
O'er twelve degrees his ribs gigantic bend,
And many a league his leathern jaws extend;
Half fish, beneath, his scaly volutes spread,
And vegetable plumage crests his head;
Huge fields of air his wrinkled skin receives
From panting gills, wide lungs, and waving leaves.
Then with dread throes subsides his bloated form:
His shriek the thunder, and his sigh the storm.
Oft high in heaven the hissing Demon wins
His towering course, upborne on winnowing fins;
Steers, with expanded eye and gaping mouth,
His mass enormous to the affrighted South;
Spreads o'er the shuddering Line his shadowy limbs,
And frost and famine follow as he swims.
Sylphs! round his cloud-built couch your bands array,
And mould the monster to your gentle sway;
Charm with soft tones, with tender touches check;
Bend to your golden yoke his willing neck;
With silver curb his yielding teeth restrain,
And give to Kirwan's hand the silken rein.
Pleased shall the sage, the dragon-wings between,
Bend o'er discordant climes his eye serene;
With Lapland breezes cool Arabian vales,
And call to Hindustan antarctic gales;
Adorn with wreathed ears Kamchatka's brows,
And scatter roses on Zealandic snows.
Earth's wondering zones the genial seasons share,
And nations hail him 'Monarch of the Air'.

X. i "Sylphs! as you hover on ethereal wing,
Brood the green children of parturient Spring!
Where in their bursting cells my embryons rest,
I charge you, guard the vegetable nest;
Count with nice eye the myriad seeds that swell
Each vaulted womb of husk, or pod, or shell;
Feed with sweet juices, clothe with downy hair,
Or hang inshrined their little orbs in air.

" So, late descry'd by Herschel's piercing sight,
Hang the bright squadrons of the twinkling Night:
Ten thousand marshall'd stars, a silver zone,
Effuse their blended lustres round her throne.
Suns call to suns, in lucid clouds conspire[51],
And light exterior skies with golden fire.
Resistless rolls the illimitable sphere,
And one great circle forms the unmeasured year.
Roll on, ye Stars! exult in youthful prime,
Mark with bright curves the printless steps of Time.
Near and more near your beamy cars approach,
And lessening orbs on lessening orbs encroach.
Flowers of the sky! ye too to age must yield,
Frail as your silken sisters of the field!
Star after star from heaven's high arch shall rush,
Suns sink on suns, and systems systems crush;
Headlong, extinct, to one dark centre fall,
And Death and Night and Chaos mingle all!
Till o'er the wreck, emerging from the storm,
Immortal Nature lifts her changeful form,
Mounts from her funeral pyre on wings of flame,
And soars and shines, another and the same.

ii " Lo! on each seed within its slender rind
Life's golden threads in endless circles wind:
Maze within maze the lucid webs are roll'd,
And, as they burst, the living flame unfold.
The pulpy acorn, ere it swells, contains
The oak's vast branches in its milky veins,
Each ravell'd bud, fine film, and fibre-line
Traced with nice pencil on the small design.
The young Narcissus, in its bulb compress'd,
Cradles a second nestling on its breast,
In whose fine arms a younger embryon lies,
Folds its thin leaves, and shuts its floret-eyes.
Grain within grain successive harvests dwell,
And boundless forests slumber in a shell.
So yon grey precipice and ivy'd towers,
Long winding meads, and intermingled bowers,
Green files of poplars, o'er the lake that bow,
And glimmering wheel which rolls and foams below,
In one bright point with nice distinction lie
Planed[52] on the moving tablet of the eye.

[51] i.e. come together in constellations [ed.]
[52] i.e. formed on the focal plane of the eye [ed.]

So, fold on fold, Earth's wavy plains extend,
And, sphere in sphere, its hidden strata bend.
Incumbent Spring her beamy plumes expands
O'er restless oceans and impatient lands,
With genial lustres warms the mighty ball,
And the Great Seed evolves, disclosing all.
Life buds or breathes from Indus to the Poles,
And the vast surface kindles, as it rolls!

iii " Come, ye soft Sylphs! who sport on Latian land,
Come, sweet-lipp'd Zephyr, and Favonius bland!
Teach the fine seed, instinct with life, to shoot
On Earth's cold bosom its descending root;
With pith elastic stretch its rising stem,
Part the twin lobes, expand the throbbing gem[53];
Clasp in your airy arms the aspiring plume,
Fan with your balmy breath its kindling bloom,
Each widening scale and bursting film unfold,
Swell the green cup, and tint the flower with gold;
While in bright veins the silvery sap ascends,
And refluent blood in milky eddies bends;
While, spread in air, the leaves respiring play,
Or drink the golden quintessence of day.
So from his shell on Delta's shower-less isle
Bursts into life the monster of the Nile:
First in translucent lymph, with cobweb-threads,
The brain's fine floating tissue swells and spreads;
Nerve after nerve the glistening spine descends,
The red heart dances, the aorta bends;
Through each new gland the purple current glides,
New veins meandering drink the refluent tides;
Edge over edge expands the hardening scale,
And sheathes his slimy skin in silver mail.
Erewhile, emerging from the brooding sand,
With tiger-paw he prints the brineless strand;
High on the flood with speckled bosom swims,
Helm'd with broad tail, and oar'd with giant limbs;
Rolls his fierce eye-balls, clasps his iron claws,
And champs with gnashing teeth his massy jaws.
Old Nilus sighs along his cane-crown'd shores,
And swarthy Memphis trembles, and adores.

53 first bud [JD]

XI “ Come, ye soft Sylphs! who fan the Paphian groves,
And bear on sportive wings the callow Loves,
Call with sweet whisper, in each gale that blows,
The slumbering Snowdrop from her long repose;
Charm the pale Primrose from her clay-cold bed;
Unveil the bashful Violet’s tremulous head,
While from her bud the playful Tulip breaks,
And young Carnations peep with blushing cheeks.
Bid the closed petals from nocturnal cold
The virgin style in silken curtains fold.
Shake into viewless air the morning dews,
And wave in light their iridescent hues;
While from on high the bursting anthers trust
To the mild breezes their prolific dust;
Or bend in rapture o’er the central Fair,
Love out their hour, and leave their lives in air.
So in his silken sepulchre the worm,
Warm’d with new life, unfolds his larva-form;
Erewhile aloft in wanton circles moves,
And woos on Hymen-wings his velvet loves.

XII. i “ If prouder branches with exuberance rude
Point their green gems, their barren shoots protrude,
Wound them, ye Sylphs! with little knives, or bind
A wiry ringlet round the swelling rind;
Bisect with chisel fine the root below,
Or bend to earth the inhospitable bough.
So shall each germ[54] with new prolific power
Delay the leaf-bud, and expand the flower.
Closed in the style the tender pith shall end,
The lengthening wood in circling stamens bend;
The smoother rind its soft embroidery spread
In vaulted petals o’er their fertile bed;
While the rough bark, in circling mazes roll’d,
Forms the green cup with many a wrinkled fold;
And each small bud-scale spreads its foliage hard
Firm round the callow germ, a floral guard.

ii “ Where cruder juices swell the leafy vein,
Stint the young germ, the tender blossom stain;
On each lopp’d shoot a foster-scion[55] bind,
Pith press’d to pith, and rind applied to rind.

---

54 sprouting seed [JD]
55 i.e. grafted branch [ed.]

So shall the trunk with loftier crest ascend,
And wide in air its happier arms extend;
Nurse the new buds, admire the leaves unknown,
And, blushing, bend with fruitage not its own.

" Thus when in holy triumph Aaron trod,
And offer'd on the shrine his mystic rod,
First a new bark its silken tissue weaves;
New buds emerging widen into leaves;
Fair fruits protrude, enascent flowers expand,
And blush and tremble round the living wand.

XIII. i " Sylphs! on each oak-bud wound the wormy galls
With pigmy spears, or crush the venom'd balls;
Fright the green locust from his foamy bed;
Unweave the caterpillar's gluey thread;
Chase the fierce earwig, scare the bloated toad;
Arrest the snail upon his slimy road;
Arm with sharp thorns the sweet-briar's tender wood,
And dash the cynips from her damask bud;
Steep in ambrosial dews the woodbine's bells,
And drive the night-moth from her honey'd cells.
Go where the humming-bird, in Chile's bowers,
On murmuring pinions robs the pendent flowers,
Seeks where fine pores their dulcet balm distil,
And sucks the treasure with proboscis-bill.
Fair Cyprepedia with successful guile
Knits her smooth brow, extinguishes her smile:
A spider's bloated paunch and jointed arms
Hide her fine form and mask her blushing charms.
In ambush sly the mimic warrior lies,
And on quick wing the panting plunderer flies.

ii " Shield the young harvest from devouring blight,
The smut's dark poison and the mildew white,
Deep-rooted mould and ergot's horn uncouth,
And break the canker's desolating tooth.
First in one point the festering wound confined
Mines unperceived beneath the shrivell'd rind;
Then climbs the branches with increasing strength,
Spreads as they spread, and lengthens with their length.
Thus the slight wound ingraved on glass unneal'd
Runs in white lines along the lucid field:
Crack follows crack, to laws elastic just,
And the frail fabric shivers into dust.

XIV. i

“ Sylphs! if with morn destructive Eurus springs,
Oh! clasp the Harebell with your velvet wings;
Screen with thick leaves the Jasmine as it blows,
And shake the white rime from the shuddering Rose,
Whilst Amaryllis turns with graceful ease
Her blushing beauties, and eludes the breeze.
Sylphs! if at noon the Fritillary droops,
With drops nectareous hang her nodding cups;
Thin clouds of gossamer in air display,
And hide the vale’s chaste Lily from the ray;
Whilst Erythrina o’er her tender flower
Bends all her leaves and braves the sultry hour.
Shield, when cold Hesper sheds his dewy light,
Mimosa’s soft sensations from the night;
Fold her thin foliage, close her timid flowers,
And with ambrosial slumbers guard her bowers;
O’er each warm wall while Cerea flings her arms,
And wastes on Night’s dull eye a blaze of charms.

ii

“ Round her tall elm with dewy fingers twine
The gadding tendrils of the adventurous vine;
From arm to arm in gay festoons suspend
Her fragrant flowers, her graceful foliage bend;
Swell with sweet juice her vermil orbs, and feed,
Shrined in transparent pulp, her pearly seed.
Hang round the orange all her silver bells,
And guard her fragrance with Hesperian spells;
Bud after bud her polish’d leaves unfold,
And load her branches with successive gold.
So the learn’d alchemist exulting sees
Rise, in his bright matrass[56], Diana’s trees;
Drop after drop, with just delay he pours
The red-fumed acid on Potosi’s ores;
With sudden flash the fierce bullitions[57] rise,
And wide in air the gas phlogistic flies;
Slow shoot, at length, in many a brilliant mass
Metallic roots across the netted glass;
Branch after branch extend their silver stems,
Bud into gold, and blossom into gems.

“ So sits enthroned in vegetable pride
Imperial Kew, by Thames’s glittering side;

---

56 chemical flask [ed.]
57 act or state of boiling [JD]

Obedient sails from realms unfurrow'd bring
For her the unnamed progeny of Spring.
Attendant Nymphs her dulcet mandates hear,
And nurse in fostering arms the tender Year;
Plant the young bulb, inhume the living seed,
Prop the weak stem, the erring tendril lead;
Or fan in glass-built fanes the stranger flowers
With milder gales, and steep with warmer showers.
Delighted Thames through tropic umbrage[58] glides,
And flowers antarctic bending o'er his tides;
Drinks the new tints, the sweets unknown inhales,
And calls the sons of science to his vales.
In one bright point, admiring Nature eyes
The fruits and foliage of discordant skies,
Twines the gay floret with the fragrant bough,
And bends the wreath round George's royal brow.
Sometimes, retiring from the public weal,
One tranquil hour the royal partners steal;
Through glades exotic pass with step sublime,
Or mark the growths of Britain's happier clime.
With beauty blossom'd, and with virtue blazed,
Mark the fair scions that themselves have raised;
Sweet blooms the rose, the towering oak expands,
The grace and guard of Britain's golden lands.

XV "Sylphs! who, round Earth on purple pinions borne,
Attend the radiant chariot of the morn;
Lead the gay Hours along the ethereal height,
And on each dun meridian shower the light.
Sylphs! who from realms of equatorial day
To climes that shudder in the polar ray,
From zone to zone pursue on shifting wing
The bright perennial journey of the Spring.
Bring my rich balms from Mecca's hallow'd glades;
Sweet flowers that glitter in Arabia's shades;
Fruits, whose fair forms in bright succession glow,
Gilding the banks of Arno, or of Po;
Each leaf, whose fragrant steam with ruby lip
Gay China's nymphs from pictur'd vases sip;
Each spicy rind which sultry India boasts,
Scenting the night-air round her breezy coasts;
Roots, whose bold stems in bleak Siberia blow,
And gem with many a tint the eternal snow;

[58] i.e. foliage [ed.]

Barks, whose broad umbrage high in ether waves
O'er Andes's steeps, and hides his golden caves;
And, where yon oak extends his dusky shoots
Wide o'er the rill that bubbles from his roots,
Beneath whose arms, protected from the storm,
A turf-built altar rears its rustic form;
Sylphs! with religious hands fresh garlands twine,
And deck with lavish pomp Hygeia's shrine.

" Call with loud voice the sisterhood that dwell
On floating cloud, wide wave, or bubbling well;
Stamp with charm'd foot, convoke the alarmed Gnomes
From golden beds and adamantine domes;
Each from her sphere with beckoning arm invite,
Curl'd with red flame the vestal Forms of light.
Close all your spotted wings, in lucid ranks
Press with your bending knees the crowded banks,
Cross your meek arms, incline your wreathed brows,
And win the Goddess with unwearied vows.
Oh wave, Hygeia! o'er Britannia's throne
Thy serpent-wand, and mark it for thy own;
Lead round her breezy coasts thy guardian trains,
Her nodding forests and her waving plains;
Shed o'er her peopled realms thy beamy smile,
And with thy airy temple crown her isle!"

The Goddess ceased and, calling from afar
The wandering Zephyrs, joins them to her car;
Mounts with light bound and, graceful as she bends,
Whirls the long lash, the flexile rein extends.
On whispering wheels the silver axle slides,
Climbs into air and cleaves the crystal tides.
Burst from its pearly chains, her amber hair
Streams o'er her ivory shoulders, buoy'd in air;
Swells her white veil, with ruby clasp confined
Round her fair brow, and undulates behind.
The lessening coursers rise in spiral rings,
Pierce the slow-sailing clouds, and stretch their shadowy wings.

End of Canto Four

Part Two

THE LOVES OF THE PLANTS

(A Linnaean Taxonomy)

Canto One

Descend, ye hovering Sylphs! aerial quires,
And sweep with little hands your silver lyres;
With fairy footsteps print your grassy rings,
Ye Gnomes! accordant to the tinkling strings;
While in soft notes I tune to oaten reed
Gay hopes and amorous sorrows of the mead:
From giant oaks that wave their branches dark,
To the dwarf moss that clings upon their bark,
What Beaux and Beauties crowd the gaudy groves
And woo and win their vegetable Loves.
How snowdrops cold, and blue-eyed harebells, blend
Their tender tears, as o'er the stream they bend;
The love-sick violet, and the primrose pale,
Bow their sweet heads and whisper to the gale;
With secret sighs the virgin lily droops,
And jealous cowslips hang their tawny cups.
How the young rose, in beauty's damask pride,
Drinks the warm blushes of his bashful bride;
With honey'd lips enamour'd woodbines meet,
Clasp with fond arms and mix their kisses sweet.

Stay thy soft-murmuring waters, gentle rill;
Hush! whispering winds; ye rustling leaves, be still!
Rest, silver butterflies, your quivering wings;
Alight, ye beetles, from your airy rings;
Ye painted moths, your gold-eyed plumage furl,
Bow your wide horns, your spiral trunks uncurl;
Glitter, ye glow-worms, on your mossy beds;
Descend, ye spiders, on your lengthen'd threads;
Slide here, ye horned snails with varnish'd shells;
Ye bee-nymphs, listen in your waxen cells!

Botanic Muse! who in this latter age
Led by your airy hand the Swedish sage[1];

[1] i.e. Carolus Linnaeus [ed.]

**Bade his keen eye your secret haunts explore,
On dewy dell, high wood, and winding shore;
Say on each leaf how tiny Graces dwell;
How laugh the Pleasures in a blossom's bell;
How insect Loves arise on cobweb wings,
Aim their light shafts and point their little stings.**

**" First the tall Canna lifts his curled brow
Erect to heaven, and plights his nuptial vow;
The virtuous pair, in milder regions born,
Dread the rude blast of autumn's icy morn;
Round the chill Fair he folds his crimson vest,
And clasps the timorous Beauty to his breast.**

**" Thy love, Callitriche[2], *two* virgins share,
Smit with thy starry eye and radiant hair;
On the green margin sits the youth, and laves
His floating train of tresses in the waves;
Sees his fair features paint the streams that pass,
And bends for ever o'er the watery glass.**

**" *Two* brother swains, of Collin's gentle name,
The same their features and their forms the same,
With rival love for fair Collinia[3] sigh,
Knit the dark brow, and roll the unsteady eye.
With sweet concern the pitying Beauty mourns,
And soothes with smiles the gentle pair, by turns.**

**" Sweet blooms Genista[4] in the myrtle shade,
And *ten* fond brothers woo the haughty maid.**

**" *Two* knights before thy fragrant altar bend,
Adored Melissa![5] and *two* squires attend.**

**" Meadia's[6] soft chains *five* suppliant Beaux confess,
And hand in hand the laughing Belle address.
Alike to all she bows with wanton air,
Rolls her dark eye and waves her golden hair.**

---

[2] fine-hair
[3] Collinsonia
[4] dyer's broom
[5] balm
[6] American cowslip

" Woo'd with long care, Curcuma[7], cold and shy,
Meets her fond husband with averted eye;
Four beardless youths the obdurate Beauty move
With soft attentions of Platonic love.

" With vain desires the pensive Alcea[8] burns,
And, like sad Eloisa, loves and mourns.

" The freckled Iris owns a fiercer flame,
And *three* unjealous husbands wed the dame.

" Cupressus dark disdains his dusky bride:
One dome contains them, but *two* beds divide.

" The proud Osyris[9] flies his angry Fair:
Two houses hold the fashionable pair.

" With strange deformity Plantago[10] treads,
A monster-birth! and lifts his hundred heads.
Yet with soft love a gentle Belle he charms,
And clasps the Beauty in his hundred arms.
So hapless Desdemona, fair and young,
Won by Othello's captivating tongue,
Sigh'd o'er each strange and piteous tale, distress'd,
And sunk enamour'd on his sooty breast.

" *Two* gentle shepherds and their sister-wives
With thee, Anthoxa![11] lead ambrosial lives:
Where the wide heath in purple pride extends,
And scatter'd furze its golden lustre blends,
Closed in a green recess (unenvy'd lot!)
The blue smoke rises from their turf-built cot;
Bosom'd in fragrance blush their infant train,
Eye the warm sun, or drink the silver rain.

" The fair Osmunda[12] seeks the silent dell,
The ivy canopy and dripping cell.
There hid in shades *clandestine* rites approves,
Till the green progeny betrays her loves.

---

[7] turmeric
[8] double hollyhock
[9] i.e. Oxyria, mountain sorrel [ed.]
[10] rose plantain
[11] Anthoxanthum, vernal grass
[12] fern [ed.]

" With charms despotic fair Chondrilla reigns
O'er the soft hearts of *five* fraternal swains:
If sighs the changeful Nymph, alike they mourn,
And if she smiles, with rival raptures burn.
So, tuned in unison, Eolian lyre!
Sounds in sweet symphony thy kindred wire:
Now, gently swept by Zephyr's vernal wings,
Sink in soft cadences thy love-sick strings;
And now with mingling chords and voices higher
Peal the full anthems of the aerial choir.

" *Five* Sister-Nymphs to join Diana's train
With thee, fair Lychnis![13] vow (but vow in vain).
Beneath one roof resides the virgin band,
Flies the fond swain, and scorns his offer'd hand.
But when soft Hours on breezy pinions move,
And smiling May attunes her lute to love,
Each wanton Beauty, trick'd in all her grace,
Shakes the bright dew-drops from her blushing face,
In gay undress displays her rival charms,
And calls her wondering lovers to her arms.

" When the young Hours, amid her tangled hair
Wove the fresh rose-bud and the lily fair,
Proud Gloriosa[14] led *three* chosen swains:
The blushing captives of her virgin chains.
When Time's rude hand a bark of wrinkles spread
Round her weak limbs, and silver'd o'er her head,
Three other youths her riper years engage,
The flatter'd victims of her wily age!
So, in her wane of beauty, Ninon won
With fatal smiles her gay unconscious son.
Clasp'd in his arms she own'd a mother's name:
'Desist, rash youth! restrain your impious flame!
First on that bed your infant form was press'd,
Born by my throes and nurtured at my breast.'
Back as from death he sprung, with wild amaze
Fierce on the fair he fix'd his ardent gaze;
Dropp'd on one knee, his frantic arms outspread,
And stole a guilty glance toward the bed;
Then breathed from quivering lips a whisper'd vow,
And bent on heaven his pale repentant brow:

---

[13] campion [ed.]
[14] Gloriosa superba

'Thus, thus!' he cried, and plunged the furious dart,
And life and love gush'd mingled from his heart.

" The fell Silene[15] and her sisters fair,
Skill'd in destruction, spread the viscous snare.
The harlot-band *ten* lofty bravoes[16] screen,
And frowning guard the magic nets unseen.
Haste glittering nations, tenants of the air,
Oh steer from hence your viewless course afar!
If with soft words, sweet blushes, nods and smiles,
The *three* dread sirens lure you to their toils,
Limed by their art, in vain you point your stings;
In vain the efforts of your whirring wings!
Go, seek your gilded mates and infant hives,
Nor taste the honey purchased with your lives!

" When heaven's high vault condensing clouds deform,
Fair Amaryllis flies the incumbent storm,
Seeks with unsteady step the shelter'd vale,
And turns her blushing beauties from the gale.
***Six* rival youths, with soft concern impress'd,**
Calm all her fears and charm her cares to rest.
So shines at eve the sun-illumined fane,
Lifts its bright cross and waves its golden vane;
From every breeze the polish'd axle turns,
And high in air the dancing meteor burns.

" *Four* of the giant brood with Ilex[17] stand;
Each grasps a thousand arrows in his hand.
A thousand steely points on every scale
Form the bright terrors of his bristly mail.
(So armed, immortal Moore uncharm'd the spell,
And slew the wily dragon of the well.)
Sudden with rage their *injured* bosoms burn,
Retort the insult or the wound return.
***Unwrong'd* as gentle as the breeze that sweeps**
The unbending harvests or undimpled deeps,
They guard the kings of Needwood's wide domains,
Their sister-wives and fair infantine trains;
Lead the lone pilgrim through the trackless glade,
Or guide in leafy wilds the wandering maid.

---

[15] catchfly
[16] those who murder for hire [JD]
[17] holly

" So Wright's bold pencil from Vesuvio's height
Hurls his red lavas to the troubled night;
From Calpe starts the intolerable flash,
Skies burst in flames, and blazing oceans dash;
Or bids in sweet repose his shades recede,
Winds the still vale and slopes the velvet mead;
On the pale stream expiring Zephyrs sink,
And moonlight sleeps upon its hoary brink.

" Gigantic Nymph! the fair Kleinhovia reigns,
The grace and terror of Orixa's[18] plains:
O'er her warm cheek the blush of beauty swims,
And nerves Herculean bend her sinewy limbs.
With frolic eye she views the affrighted throng,
And shakes the meadows as she towers along;
With playful violence displays her charms,
And bears her trembling lovers in her arms. [19]
So fair Thalestris shook her plumy crest,
And bound in rigid mail her jutting breast;
Poised her long lance amid the walks of war,
And Beauty thunder'd from Bellona's car.
Greece arm'd in vain: her captive heroes wove
The chains of conquest with the wreaths of love.

" When o'er the cultured lawns and dreary wastes
Retiring Autumn flings her howling blasts;
Bends in tumultuous waves the struggling woods,
And showers their leafy honours on the floods;
In withering heaps collects the flowery spoil,
And each chill insect sinks beneath the soil;
Quick flies fair Tulipa the loud alarms,
And folds her infant closer in her arms;
In some lone cave, secure pavilion, lies,
And waits the courtship of serener skies.
So, six cold moons the dormouse charm'd to rest,
Indulgent Sleep! beneath thy eider breast,
In fields of fancy climbs the kernell'd groves,
Or shares the golden harvests with his Loves.

" Then bright from earth, amid the troubled sky,
Ascends fair Colchica[20] with radiant eye;

---

[18] i.e. Orissa, N.E.India [ed.]
[19] The line numbering here reflects an editorial error in the 1791 edition. [ed.]
[20] Colchicum autumnale, autumnal meadow-saffron

Warms the cold bosom of the hoary year
And lights with beauty's blaze the dusky sphere.
***Three* blushing maids the intrepid Nymph attend,**
And *six* gay youths, enamour'd train! defend.
So shines with silver guards the Georgian star[21],
And drives on night's blue arch his glittering car;
Hangs o'er the billowy clouds his lucid form,
Wades through the mist and dances in the storm.

" Great Helianthus[22] guides o'er twilight plains
In gay solemnity his dervish-trains;
Marshall'd in *fives* each gaudy band proceeds,
Each gaudy band a plumed lady leads;
With zealous step he climbs the upland lawn,
And bows in homage to the rising dawn;
Imbibes with eagle-eye the golden ray,
And watches, as it moves, the orb of day.

" Queen of the marsh, imperial Drosera[23] treads
Rush-fringed banks and moss-embroider'd beds.
Redundant folds of glossy silk surround
Her slender waist and trail upon the ground.
***Five* sister-nymphs collect, with graceful ease,**
Or spread the floating purple to the breeze;
And *five* fair youths with duteous love comply
With each soft mandate of her moving eye.
As with sweet grace her snowy neck she bows,
A zone of diamonds trembles round her brows:
Bright shines the silver halo as she turns,
And, as she steps, the living lustre burns.

" Fair Lonicera[24] prints the dewy lawn,
And decks with brighter blush the vermil dawn;
Winds round the shadowy rocks and pansied vales,
And scents with sweeter breath the summer gales.
With artless grace and native ease she charms,
And bears the Horn of Plenty in her arms.
***Five* rival swains their tender cares unfold,**
And watch with eye askance the treasured gold.

---

21 Uranus, discovered by William Herschel in 1781, first named after George III [ed.]
22 sunflower
23 sundew
24 Lonicera caprifolium, honeysuckle

" Where rears huge Tenerif his azure crest,
Aspiring Draba[25] builds her eagle-nest;
Her pendent eyry icy caves surround,
Where erst volcanoes mined the rocky ground.
Pleased, round the fair *four* rival lords ascend
The shaggy steeps; *two* menial youths attend.
High in the setting ray the Beauty stands,
And her tall shadow waves on distant lands.

" Oh! stay, bright habitant of air, alight,
Ambitious Visca[26], from thy angel-flight!
Scorning the sordid soil, aloft she springs,
Shakes her white plume and claps her golden wings;
High o'er the fields of boundless Ether roves,
And seeks amid the clouds her soaring Loves!

" Stretch'd on her mossy couch, in trackless deeps,
Queen of the coral groves, Zostera[27] sleeps:
The silvery seaweed matted round her bed,
And distant surges murmuring o'er her head.
High in the flood her azure dome ascends:
The crystal arch on crystal columns bends;
Roof'd with translucent shell the turrets blaze,
And far in ocean dart their colour'd rays;
O'er the white floor successive shadows move,
As rise and break the ruffled waves above.
Around the Nymph her mermaid-trains repair,
And weave with orient pearl her radiant hair.
With rapid fins she cleaves the watery way,
Shoots like a silver meteor up to day;
Sounds a loud conch, convokes a scaly band
(Her sea-born lovers) and ascends the strand.

" E'en round the Pole the flames of love aspire,
And icy bosoms feel the *secret* fire!
Cradled in snow, and fann'd by Arctic air,
Shines, gentle Barometz![28] thy golden hair.
Rooted in earth each cloven hoof descends,
And round and round her flexile neck she bends;
Crops the gray coral moss and hoary thyme,
Or laps with rosy tongue the melting rime;

---

[25] Draba alpina, Alpine whitlow-grass
[26] Viscum, mistletoe
[27] grass-wrack
[28] Tartarian lamb

Eyes with mute tenderness her distant dam,
Or seems to bleat, a *vegetable lamb*.
So, warm and buoyant in his oily mail,
Gambols on seas of ice the unwieldy whale;
Wide-waving fins round floating islands urge
His bulk gigantic through the troubled surge.
With hideous yawn the flying shoals he seeks,
Or clasps with fringe of horn his massy cheeks;
Lifts o'er the tossing wave his nostrils bare,
And spouts pellucid columns into air.
The silvery arches catch the setting beams,
And transient rainbows tremble o'er the streams.

" Weak with nice sense, the chaste Mimosa[29] stands;
From each rude touch withdraws her timid hands.
Oft, as light clouds o'erpass the summer-glade,
Alarm'd she trembles at the moving shade,
And feels, alive through all her tender form,
The whisper'd murmurs of the gathering storm;
Shuts her sweet eye-lids to approaching night,
And hails with freshen'd charms the rising light.
Veil'd, with gay decency and modest pride,
Slow to the mosque she moves, an eastern bride;
There her soft vows unceasing love record,
Queen of the bright seraglio of her lord.
So sinks or rises with the changeful hour
The liquid silver in its glassy tower;
So turns the needle to the Pole it loves,
With fine librations quivering, as it moves.

" All wan and shivering in the leafless glade,
The sad Anemone reclined her head:
Grief on her cheeks had paled the roseate hue,
And her sweet eyelids dropp'd with pearly dew.
'See, from bright regions borne on odorous gales
The swallow, herald of the summer, sails.
Breathe, gentle Air! from cherub-lips impart
Thy balmy influence to my anguish'd heart.
Thou whose soft voice calls forth the tender blooms,
Whose pencil paints them, and whose breath perfumes,
Oh! chase the Fiend of Frost with leaden mace,
Who seals in death-like sleep my hapless race;
Melt his hard heart, release his iron hand,
And give my ivory petals to expand.

29 sensitive plant

So may each bud that decks the brow of Spring
Shed all its incense on thy wafting wing!'
To her fond prayer propitious Zephyr yields;
Sweeps on his sliding shell through azure fields;
O'er her fair mansion waves his whispering wand,
And gives her ivory petals to expand.
Gives with new life her filial train to rise
And hail with kindling smiles the genial skies.
So shines the Nymph in beauty's blushing pride,
When Zephyr wafts her deep calash[30] aside;
Tears with rude kiss her bosom's gauzy veil,
And flings the fluttering kerchief to the gale.
So bright, the folding canopy undrawn,
Glides the gilt landau o'er the velvet lawn;
Of Beaux and Belles displays the glittering throng,
And soft airs fan them as they roll along.

" Where frowning Snowdon bends his dizzy brow
O'er Conway, listening to the surge below,
Retiring Lichen climbs the topmost stone
And drinks the aerial solitude alone.
Bright shine the stars unnumber'd o'er her head,
And the cold moon-beam gilds her flinty bed,
While round the rifted rocks hoarse whirlwinds breathe,
And dark with thunder sail the clouds beneath.
The steepy path her plighted swain pursues,
And tracks her light steps o'er the imprinted dews.
Delighted Hymen gives his torch to blaze,
Winds round the crags and lights the mazy ways;
Sheds o'er their *secret* vows his influence chaste,
And decks with roses the admiring waste.

" High in the front of heaven when Sirius glares,
And o'er Britannia shakes his fiery hairs;
When no soft shower descends, no dew distils,
Her wave-worn channels dry, and mute her rills;
When droops the sickening herb, the blossom fades,
And parch'd earth gapes beneath the withering glades,
With languid step fair Dypsaca[31] retreats.
'Fall, gentle dews!' the fainting Nymph repeats,
Seeks the low dell, and in the sultry shade
Invokes in vain the Naiads to her aid.

---

30 head dress [JD]
31 teasel

Four sylvan youths in crystal goblets bear
The untasted treasure to the grateful Fair:
Pleased from their hands with modest grace she sips,
And the cool wave reflects her coral lips.

" With nice selection, modest Rubia[32] blends
Her vermil dyes, and o'er the cauldron bends:
Warm mid the rising steam the Beauty glows,
As blushes in a mist the dewy rose.
With chemic art *four* favour'd youths, aloof,
Stain the white fleece or stretch the tinted woof;
O'er Age's cheek the warmth of youth diffuse,
Or deck the pale-ey'd Nymph in roseate hues.
So when Medea to exulting Greece
From plunder'd Colchis bore the golden fleece,
On the loud shore a magic pile she raised:
The cauldron bubbled, and the faggots blazed.
Pleased, on the boiling wave old Aeson swims,
And feels new vigour stretch his swelling limbs;
Through his thrill'd nerves forgotten ardours dart,
And warmer eddies circle round his heart;
With softer fires his kindling eye-balls glow,
And darker tresses wanton round his brow.

[" Where Java's isle, horizon'd with the floods, (i)[33]
Lifts to the sky her canopy of woods,
Pleased Epidendra[34] climbs the waving pines,
And high in heaven the intrepid Beauty shines:
Gives to the tropic breeze her radiant hair,
Drinks the bright shower, and feeds upon the air.
Her brood delighted stretch their callow wings,
As poised aloft their pendent cradle swings;
Eye the warm sun, the spicy Zephyr breathe,
And gaze unenvious on the world beneath.] (x)

" As dash the waves on India's breezy strand,
Her flush'd cheek press'd upon her lily hand,
Vallisner[35] sits, upturns her tearful eyes,
Calls her lost lover, and upbraids the skies.
For him she breathes the silent sigh forlorn
Each setting day; for him each rising morn:

---

[32] madder
[33] These ten lines are inserted in the 1824 edition. [ed.]
[34] Epidendrum flos aeris
[35] Vallisneria

'Bright Orbs, that light yon high ethereal plain,
Or bathe your radiant tresses in the main;
Pale Moon, that silver'st o'er Night's sable brow,
(For ye were witness to his parting vow!)
Ye shelving rocks, dark waves, and sounding shore,
(Ye echoed sweet the tender words he swore!)
Can stars or seas the sails of love retain?
Oh, guide my wanderer to my arms again!'

" Her buoyant skiff intrepid Ulva[36] guides,
And seeks her lord amid the trackless tides.
Her *secret* vows the Cyprian Queen approves,
And hovering halcyons guard her Infant-Loves:
Each in his floating cradle round they throng,
And dimpling ocean bears the fleet along.
Thus o'er the waves, which gently bend and swell,
Fair Galatea steers her silver shell.
Her playful dolphins stretch the silken rein,
Hear her sweet voice, and glide along the main.
As round the wild meandering coast she moves
By gushing rills, rude cliffs, and nodding groves,
Each by her pine the Wood-nymphs wave their locks,
And wondering Naiads peep amid the rocks;
Pleased trains of Mermaids rise from coral cells;
Admiring Tritons sound their twisted shells;
Charm'd, o'er the car pursuing Cupids sweep,
Their snow-white pinions twinkling in the deep;
And, as the lustre of her eye she turns,
Soft sighs the Gale, and amorous Ocean burns.

" On Dove's green brink the fair Tremella[37] stood
And view'd her playful image in the flood;
To each rude rock, lone dell, and echoing grove,
Sung the sweet sorrows of her *secret* love.
'Oh, stay! Return!' along the sounding shore
Cried the sad Naiads. She return'd no more!
Now girt with clouds the sullen Evening frown'd,
And withering Eurus swept along the ground;
The misty moon withdrew her horned light,
And sunk with Hesper in the skirt of night.
No dim electric streams (the northern dawn)
With meek effulgence quiver'd o'er the lawn;

---

[36] bladder-wrack [ed.]
[37] a genus of fungus [ed.]

No star benignant shot one transient ray
To guide or light the wanderer on her way.
Round the dark crags the murmuring whirlwinds blow,
Woods groan above, and waters roar below.
As o'er the steeps with pausing foot she moves,
The pitying Dryads shriek amid their groves.
She flies, she stops, she pants, she looks behind,
And hears a demon howl in every wind.
As the bleak blast unfurls her fluttering vest,
Cold beats the snow upon her shuddering breast;
Through her numb'd limbs the chill sensations dart,
And the keen ice-bolt trembles at her heart.
'I sink, I fall! Oh, help me, help!' she cries.
Her stiffening tongue the unfinish'd sound denies.
Tear after tear adown her cheek succeeds,
And pearls of ice bestrew the glittering meads;
Congealing snows her lingering feet surround,
Arrest her flight and root her to the ground.
With suppliant arms she pours the silent prayer:
Her suppliant arms hang crystal in the air.
Pellucid films her shivering neck o'erspread,
Seal her mute lips, and silver o'er her head;
Veil her pale bosom, glaze her lifted hands,
And shrined in ice the beauteous statue stands.
Dove's azure Nymphs, on each revolving year,
For fair Tremella shed the tender tear;
With rush-wove crowns in sad procession move,
And sound the sorrowing shell to hapless love."

Here paused the Muse. Across the darken'd Pole
Sail the dim clouds, the echoing thunders roll.
The trembling Wood-Nymphs, as the tempest lowers,
Lead the gay Goddess to their inmost bowers;
Hang the mute lyre the laurel shade beneath,
And round her temples bind the myrtle wreath.

Now the light swallow with her airy brood
Skims the green meadow and the dimpled flood.
Loud shrieks the lone thrush from his leafless thorn.
Th' alarmed beetle sounds his bugle-horn.
Each pendent spider winds with fingers fine
His ravell'd clew, and climbs along the line.
Gay Gnomes in glittering circles stand aloof
Beneath a spreading mushroom's fretted roof.
Swift bees returning seek their waxen cells,
And Sylphs cling quivering in the lily's bells.

Through the still air descend the genial showers,
And pearly raindrops deck the laughing flowers.

End of Canto One

Canto Two

Again the Goddess strikes the golden lyre,
And tunes to wilder notes the warbling wire.
With soft suspended step Attention moves,
And Silence hovers o'er the listening groves.
Orb within orb the charmed audience throng,
And the green vault reverberates the song.

" 'Breathe soft, ye gales!' the fair Carlina[38] cries.
'Bear on broad wings your votress to the skies.
How sweetly mutable yon orient hues,
As Morn's fair hand her opening roses strews;
How bright, when Iris, blending many a ray,
Binds in embroider'd wreath the brow of Day;
Soft, when the pendent Moon with lustres pale
O'er heaven's blue arch unfurls her milky veil;
While from the north long threads of silver light
Dart on swift shuttles o'er the tissued Night!
Breathe soft, ye Zephyrs! hear my fervent sighs:
Bear on broad wings your votress to the skies!'
Plume over plume, in long divergent lines
On whale-bone ribs, the fair mechanic joins;
Inlays with eider-down the silken strings,
And weaves in wide expanse Daedalian wings;
Round her bold sons the waving pennons binds,
And walks with angel-step upon the winds.

" So on the shoreless air the intrepid Gaul
Launch'd the vast concave of his buoyant ball.
Journeying on high, the silken castle glides
Bright as a meteor through the azure tides.
O'er towns and towers and temples wins its way,
Or mounts sublime, and gilds the vault of day.
Silent, with upturn'd eyes, unbreathing crowds
Pursue the floating wonder to the clouds,
And, flush'd with transport, or benumb'd with fear,
Watch, as it rises, the diminish'd sphere:
Now less, and less; and now a speck is seen,
And now the fleeting wrack obtrudes between!
With bended knees, raised arms, and suppliant brows,
To every shrine they breathe their mingled vows[39]:

---

[38] carline thistle
[39] 'brows...vows' - plurals adopted from the 1824 edition as syntactically better [ed.]

**'Save him, ye Saints! who o'er the good preside;
Bear him, ye winds! ye stars benignant! guide.'
The calm philosopher in ether sails,
Views broader stars, and breathes in purer gales;
Sees, like a map, in many a waving line
Round Earth's blue plains her lucid waters shine;
Sees at his feet the forky lightnings glow,
And hears innocuous thunders roar below.
Rise, great Montgolfier! urge thy venturous flight
High o'er the Moon's pale ice-reflected light;
High o'er the pearly star[40], whose beamy horn
Hangs in the east, gay harbinger of morn;
Leave the red eye of Mars on rapid wing,
Jove's silver guards, and Saturn's crystal ring;
Leave the fair beams which, issuing from afar,
Play with new lustres round the Georgian star;
Shun with strong oars the Sun's attractive throne,
The sparkling zodiac, and the milky zone
Where headlong comets, with increasing force,
Through other systems bend their blazing course.
For thee Cassiope her chair withdraws;
For thee the Bear retracts his shaggy paws.
High o'er the north thy golden orb shall roll,
And blaze eternal round the wondering Pole.
So Argo, rising from the southern main,
Lights with new stars the blue ethereal plain;
With favouring beams the mariner protects,
And the bold course, which first it steer'd, directs.**

**" Inventress of the woof, fair Lina[41] flings
The flying shuttle through the dancing strings;
Inlays the broider'd weft with flowery dyes.
Quick beat the reeds, the pedals fall and rise;
Slow from the beam the lengths of warp unwind,
And dance and nod the massy weights behind.
Taught by her labours, from the fertile soil
Immortal Isis clothed the banks of Nile;
And fair Arachne, with her rival loom,
Found undeserved a melancholy doom.
Five sister-nymphs with dewy fingers twine
The beamy flax, and stretch the fibre-line;**

---

40 i.e. the planet Venus [ed.]
41 flax

Quick eddying threads from rapid spindles reel,
Or whirl with beating foot the dizzy wheel.
Charm'd, round the busy Fair *five* shepherds press,
Praise the nice texture of their snowy dress,
Admire the artists, and the art approve,
And tell with honey'd words the tale of love.

" So now, where Derwent rolls his dusky floods
Through vaulted mountains, and a night of woods,
The nymph Gossypia[42] treads the velvet sod,
And warms with rosy smiles the watery god;
His ponderous oars to slender spindles turns,
And pours o'er massy wheels his foamy urns;
With playful charms her hoary lover wins,
And wields his trident, while the monarch spins.
First, with nice eye emerging Naiads cull
From leathery pods the vegetable wool;
With wiry teeth revolving cards release
The tangled knots and smooth the ravell'd fleece;
Next moves the iron-hand with fingers fine,
Combs the wide card and forms the eternal line;
Slow, with soft lips, the whirling can acquires
The tender skeins, and wraps in rising spires;
With quicken'd pace successive rollers move,
And these retain, and those extend, the rove[43];
Then fly the spoles, the rapid axles glow,
And slowly circumvolves the labouring wheel below.

" Papyra, throned upon the banks of Nile,
Spread her smooth leaf and waved her silver style.
The storied pyramid, the laurel'd bust,
The trophied arch, had crumbled into dust:
The sacred symbol, and the epic song
(Unknown the character, forgot the tongue)
With each unconquer'd chief or sainted maid,
Sunk undistinguished in oblivion's shade.
Sad o'er the scatter'd ruins Genius sigh'd,
And infant Arts but learn'd to lisp, and died,
Till, to astonish'd realms Papyra taught
To paint in mystic colours sound and thought.
With wisdom's voice to print the page sublime,
And mark in adamant the steps of Time.

---

[42] Gossypium, cotton plant
[43] twisted length of cotton ready for spinning [ed.]

Six favour'd youths her soft attention share,
The fond disciples of the studious Fair;
Hear her sweet voice; the golden process prove;
Gaze as they learn and, as they listen, love.
The first from Alpha to Omega joins
The letter'd tribes along the level lines;
Weighs with nice ear the vowel, liquid, surd,
And breaks in syllables the volant word.
Then forms the next upon the marshall'd plain
In deepening ranks his dexterous cipher-train,
And counts, as wheel the decimating[44] bands,
The dews of Egypt, or Arabia's sands.
And then the third on four concordant lines
Prints the lone crotchet, and the quaver joins;
Marks the gay trill, the solemn pause inscribes,
And parts with bars the undulating tribes.
Pleased, round her cane-wove throne the applauding crowd
Clapp'd their rude hands, their swarthy foreheads bow'd;
With loud acclaim, 'A present god!' they cried;
'A present god!' rebellowing shores replied.
Then peal'd at intervals, with mingled swell,
The echoing harp, shrill clarion, horn, and shell;
While Bards ecstatic, bending o'er the lyre,
Struck deeper chords, and wing'd the song with fire.
Then mark'd astronomers, with keener eyes,
The Moon's refulgent journey through the skies;
Watch'd the swift comets urge their blazing cars,
And weighed the Sun with his revolving stars.
High raised the chemists their hermetic wands
(And changing forms obey'd their waving hands);
Her treasured gold from Earth's deep chambers tore,
Or fused and harden'd her chalybeate[45] ore.
All with bent knee, from fair Papyra claim,
Wove by her hands, the wreath of deathless fame.
Exulting Genius crown'd his darling child;
The young Arts clasp'd her knees, and Virtue smiled.

" So now Delany forms her mimic bowers,
Her paper foliage and her silken flowers.
Her virgin train the tender scissors ply,
Vein the green leaf, the purple petal dye;

---

44 i.e. moving in groups of ten [ed.]
45 containing iron [ed.]

Round wiry stems the flaxen tendril bends,
Moss creeps below, and waxen fruit impends.
Cold Winter views, amid his realms of snow,
Delany's vegetable statues blow;
Smooths his stern brow, delays his hoary wing,
And eyes with wonder all the blooms of Spring.

" The gentle Lapsana[46], Nymphaea[47] fair,
And bright Calendula[48] with golden hair,
Watch with nice eye the Earth's diurnal way,
Marking her solar and sidereal day,
Her slow nutation and her varying clime,
And trace with mimic art the march of Time.
Round his light foot a magic chain they fling,
And count the quick vibrations of his wing.
First, in its brazen cell reluctant roll'd,
Bends the dark spring in many a steely fold;
On spiral brass is stretch'd the wiry thong;
Tooth urges tooth, and wheel drives wheel along;
In diamond-eyes the polish'd axles flow;
Smooth slides the hand, the balance pants below.
Round the white circlet, in relievo bold,
A serpent twines his scaly length in gold;
And brightly pencill'd on the enamell'd sphere
Live the fair trophies of the passing year.
Here Time's huge fingers grasp his giant mace,
And dash proud Superstition from her base;
Rend her strong towers and gorgeous fanes, and shed
The crumbling fragments round her guilty head.
There the gay Hours, whom wreaths of roses deck,
Lead their young trains amid the cumbrous wreck,
And, slowly purpling o'er the mighty waste,
Plant the fair growths of Science and of Taste.
While each light Moment, as it dances by
With feathery foot and pleasure-twinkling eye,
Feeds from its baby-hand, with many a kiss,
The callow nestlings of domestic bliss.

" As yon gay clouds, which canopy the skies,
Change their thin forms and lose their lucid dyes,
So the soft bloom of Beauty's vernal charms
Fades in our eyes, and withers in our arms.

---

46 nipplewort
47 white water lily
48 marigold [ed.]

Bright as the silvery plume or pearly shell,
The snow-white rose or lily's virgin bell,
The fair Helleboras[49] attractive shone,
Warm'd every sage, and every shepherd won.
Round the gay Sisters press the enamour'd bands,
And seek, with soft solicitude, their hands.
Erewhile, how changed! In dim suffusion lies
The glance divine that lighten'd in their eyes;
Cold are those lips where smiles seductive hung,
And the weak accents linger on their tongue;
Each roseate feature fades to livid green.
Disgust, with face averted, shuts the scene.

"So from his gorgeous throne, which awed the world,
The mighty monarch of Assyria hurl'd,
Sojourn'd with brutes beneath the midnight storm,
Changed by avenging Heaven in mind and form.
Prone to the earth he bends his brow superb,
Crops the young floret and the bladed herb;
Lolls his red tongue, and from the reedy side
Of slow Euphrates laps the muddy tide.
Long eagle-plumes his arching neck invest,
Steal round his arms and clasp his sharpen'd breast;
Dark brinded hairs, in bristling ranks behind,
Rise o'er his back and rustle in the wind,
Clothe his lank sides, his shrivell'd limbs surround,
And human hands with talons print the ground.
Silent in shining troops the courtier-throng
Pursue their monarch as he crawls along.
E'en Beauty pleads in vain with smiles and tears,
Nor Flattery's self can pierce his pendent ears.

"*Two* sister-nymphs[50] to Ganges's flowery brink
Bend their light steps, the lucid water drink;
Wind through the dewy rice and nodding canes
(As *eight* black eunuchs guard the sacred plains;)
With playful malice watch the scaly brood,
And shower the inebriate berries on the flood.
Stay in your crystal chambers, silver tribes!
Turn your bright eyes and shun the dangerous bribes.
The trammell'd'd[51] net with less destruction sweeps
Your curling shallows and your azure deeps;

[49] Helleborus niger, Christmas rose
[50] i.e. Menispermum, Indian berry
[51] fine-meshed net drawn through a coarse-meshed net by the fish to form a pocket [ed.]

With less deceit, the gilded fly beneath,
Lurks the fell hook unseen. To taste is death!
Dim your slow eyes, and dull your pearly coat,
Drunk on the waves your languid forms shall float;
On useless fins in giddy circles play,
And herons and otters seize you for their prey.

" So, when the Saint from Padua's graceless land
In silent anguish sought the barren strand,
High on the shatter'd beech sublime he stood;
Still'd with his waving arm the babbling flood.
'To man's dull ear,' he cried, 'I call in vain;
Hear me, ye scaly tenants of the main!'
Misshapen seals approach in circling flocks;
In dusky mail the tortoise climbs the rocks;
Torpedoes[52], sharks, rays, porpoise, dolphins, pour
Their twinkling squadrons round the glittering shore.
With tangled fins behind huge phocae[53] glide,
And whales and grampi[54] swell the distant tide.
Then kneel'd the hoary seer, to heaven address'd
His fiery eyes, and smote his sounding breast.
'Bless ye the Lord' with thundering voice he cried;
'Bless ye the Lord!' the bending shores replied.
The winds and waters caught the sacred word,
And mingling echoes shouted 'Bless the Lord!'
The listening shoals the quick contagion feel:
Pant on the floods, inebriate with their zeal;
Ope their wide jaws and bow their slimy heads,
And dash with frantic fins their foamy beds.

" Sofa'd on silk, amid her charm-built towers,
Her meads of asphodel, and amaranth[55] bowers,
Where sleep and silence guard the soft abodes,
In sullen apathy Papaver nods.
Faint o'er her couch in scintillating streams
Pass the thin forms of Fancy and of Dreams.
Froze by inchantment on the velvet ground,
Fair youths and beauteous ladies glitter round;
On crystal pedestals they seem to sigh,
Bend the meek knee and lift the imploring eye.

---

52 fish capable of giving an electric shock [ed.]
53 seals [ed.]
54 large fish of the whale kind [JD]
55 imaginary flower that never fades [JD]

**“ And now the Sorceress bares her shrivell’d hand,
And circles thrice in air her ebon wand.
Flush’d with new life, descending statues talk,
(The pliant marble softening as they walk).
With deeper sobs reviving lovers breathe;
Fair bosoms rise and soft hearts pant beneath.
With warmer lips relenting damsels speak,
And kindling blushes tinge the Parian cheek.
To viewless lutes aerial voices sing,
And hovering Loves are heard on rustling wing.
She waves her wand again! Fresh horrors seize
Their stiffening limbs, their vital currents freeze.
By each cold nymph her marble lover lies,
And iron slumbers seal their glassy eyes.
So with his dread Caduceus, Hermes led
From the dark regions of the imprison’d dead,
Or drove in silent shoals the lingering train
To night’s dull shore and Pluto’s dreary reign.**

**“ So with her waving pencil, Crewe commands
The realms of taste and fancy’s fairy lands;
Calls up with magic voice the shapes that sleep
In earth’s dark bosom or unfathom’d deep;
That shrined in air on viewless wings aspire,
Or, blazing, bathe in elemental fire.
As with nice touch her plastic hand she moves,
Rise the fine forms of Beauties, Graces, Loves:
Kneel to the fair enchantress, smile or sigh,
And fade or flourish as she turns her eye.**

**“ Fair Cista[56], rival of the rosy dawn,
Call’d her light choir and trod the dewy lawn;
Hail’d with rude melody the new-born May,
As cradled yet in April’s lap she lay:**

**1. ‘Born in yon blaze of orient sky,
Sweet May! thy radiant form unfold;
Unclose thy blue voluptuous eye,
And wave thy shadowy locks of gold.**

**2. For thee the fragrant zephyrs blow;
For thee descends the sunny shower;
The rills in softer murmurs flow,
And brighter blossoms gem the bower.**

---

[56] Cistus: flowers soon after dawn, and its petals fall later the same day [ed.]

3. Light Graces dress'd in flowery wreaths
And tiptoe Joys their hands combine;
And Love his sweet contagion breathes,
And laughing dances round thy shrine.

4. Warm with new life, the glittering throngs
On quivering fin and rustling wing
Delighted join their votive songs,
And hail thee, Goddess of the Spring.'

O'er the green brinks of Severn's oozy bed
In changeful rings her sprightly troops she led;
Pan tripp'd before, where Eudness[57] shades the mead,
And blew with glowing lip his sevenfold reed.
Emerging Naiads swell'd the jocund strain
And aped with mimic step the dancing train.
'I faint! I fall!' at noon the Beauty cried,
'Weep o'er my tomb, ye Nymphs!' and sunk and died.

" Thus when white Winter o'er the shivering clime
Drives the still snow or showers the silver rime,
As the lone shepherd o'er the dazzling rocks
Prints his steep step and guides his vagrant flocks;
Views the green holly veil'd in net-work nice,
Her vermil clusters twinkling in the ice;
Admires the lucid vales and slumbering floods,
Fantastic cataracts and crystal woods,
Transparent towns with seas of milk between,
And eyes with transport the refulgent scene.
If breaks the sunshine o'er the spangled trees,
Or flits on tepid wing the western breeze,
In liquid dews descends the transient glare,
And all the glittering pageant melts in air.

" Where Andes hides his cloud-wreath'd crest in snow,
And roots his base on burning sands below,
Cinchona[58], fairest of Peruvian maids,
To health's bright Goddess in the breezy glades
On Quito's temperate plain an altar rear'd,
Trill'd the loud hymn, the solemn prayer preferr'd;
Each balmy bulb she culled, and honey'd flower,
And hung with fragrant wreaths the sacred bower;

---

57 happiness [ed.]
58 Peruvian bark-tree (the source of quinine [ed.])

**Each pearly sea she search'd, and sparkling mine,
And piled their treasures on the gorgeous shrine.
Her suppliant voice for sickening Loxa[59] raised;
Sweet breathed the gale and bright the censer blazed.
'Divine Hygeia! on thy votaries bend
Thy angel-looks; oh, hear us, and defend!
While streaming o'er the night with baleful glare
The Star of Autumn[60] rays his misty hair,
Fierce from his fens the giant Ague springs,
And, wrapp'd in fogs, descends on vampire-wings.
Before, with shuddering limbs, cold Tremor reels,
And Fever's burning nostril dogs his heels.
Loud claps the grinning Fiend his iron hands,
Stamps with black hoof, and shouts along the lands;
Withers the damask cheek, unnerves the strong,
And drives with scorpion-lash the shrieking throng.
Oh Goddess! on thy kneeling votaries bend
Thy angel-looks. Oh, hear us, and defend!'**

**" Hygeia, leaning from the blest abodes
(The crystal mansions of the immortal gods)
Saw the sad Nymph uplift her dewy eyes,
Spread her white arms, and breathe her fervid sighs;
Call'd to her fair associates, Youth and Joy,
And shot all radiant through the glittering sky.
Loose waved behind her golden train of hair,
Her sapphire mantle swam, diffused in air.
O'er the grey matted moss and pansied sod
With step sublime the glowing Goddess trod;
Gilt with her beamy eye the conscious shade,
And with her smile celestial bless'd the maid.
'Come to my arms!' with seraph voice she cries,
'Thy vows are heard, benignant Nymph, arise!
Where yon aspiring trunks fantastic wreathe
Their mingled roots, and drink the rill beneath,
Yield to the biting axe thy sacred wood,
And strew the bitter foliage on the flood.'
In silent homage bow'd the blushing maid;**
Five **youths athletic hasten to her aid.
O'er the scarr'd hills re-echoing strokes resound,
And, headlong, forests thunder on the ground.
Round the dark roots, rent bark, and shatter'd boughs,
From ochrous beds the swelling fountain flows;**

---

59 i.e. Loja, a Spanish colony until 1830 when Ecuador, with Quito as capital, gained independence [ed.]
60 perhaps a comet [ed.]

**With streams austere its winding margin laves,
And pours from vale to vale its dusky waves.**

**" As the pale squadrons, bending o'er the brink,
View with a sigh their alter'd forms, and drink,
Slow-ebbing life with refluent crimson breaks
O'er their wan lips, and paints their haggard cheeks.
Through each fine nerve rekindling transports dart,
Light the quick eye and swell the exulting heart.**

**" Thus Israel's heaven-taught chief o'er trackless sands
Led to the sultry rock his murmuring bands.
Bright o'er his brows the forky radiance blazed,
And high in air the rod divine he raised.
Wide yawns the cliff! Amid the thirsty throng
Rush the redundant waves and shine along.
With gourds and shells and helmets press the bands,
Ope their parch'd lips and spread their eager hands;
Snatch their pale infants to the exuberant shower;
Kneel on the shatter'd rock and bless the almighty Power.**

**" Bolster'd with down, amid a thousand wants,
Pale Dropsy rears his bloated form, and pants.
'Quench me, ye cool pellucid rills!' he cries,
Wets his parch'd tongue and rolls his hollow eyes.
So bends tormented Tantalus to drink,
While from his lips the refluent waters shrink.
Again the rising stream his bosom laves,
And thirst consumes him 'mid circumfluent waves.**

**" Divine Hygeia, from the bending sky
Descending, listens to his piercing cry;
Assumes bright Digitalis's[61] dress and air,
Her ruby cheek, white neck, and raven hair.
Four youths protect her from the circling throng,
And like the Nymph the Goddess steps along.
O'er him she waves her serpent-wreathed wand,
Cheers with her voice, and raises with her hand;
Warms with rekindling bloom his visage wan,
And charms the shapeless monster into man.**

**" So when Contagion, with mephitic[62] breath,
And wither'd Famine urged the work of death,**

---

61 foxglove
62 stinking [JD]

Marseilles's good Bishop, London's generous Mayor,
With food and faith, with medicine, and with prayer,
Rais'd the weak head and stay'd the parting sigh,
Or with new life relumed the swimming eye.

" And now, Philanthropy! thy rays divine
Dart round the globe from Zembla to the Line.
O'er each dark prison plays the cheering light,
Like northern lustres o'er the vault of night.
From realm to realm, with cross or crescent crown'd,
Where'er mankind and misery are found,
O'er burning sands, deep waves, or wilds of snow,
Thy Howard journeying seeks the house of woe.
Down many a winding step to dungeons dank,
Where anguish wails aloud, and fetters clank;
To caves bestrew'd with many a mouldering bone,
And cells, whose echoes only learn to groan;
Where no kind bars a whispering friend disclose,
No sunbeam enters, and no zephyr blows,
He treads, inemulous of fame or wealth,
Profuse of toil and prodigal of health.
With soft assuasive eloquence expands
Power's rigid heart, and opes his clenching hands;
Leads stern-eyed Justice to the dark domains,
If not to sever, to relax the chains.
Or guides awaken'd Mercy through the gloom,
And shows the prison, sister to the tomb!
Gives to her babes the self-devoted wife;
To her fond husband, liberty and life!

" The spirits of the good, who bend from high
Wide o'er these earthly scenes their partial eye,
When first, array'd in Virtue's purest robe
They saw her Howard traversing the globe;
Saw round his brows her sun-like glory blaze
In arrowy circles of unwearied rays,
Mistook a mortal for an angel-guest,
And ask'd what seraph-foot the earth imprest.
Onward he moves! Disease and Death retire,
And murmuring Demons hate him, and admire."

Here paused the Goddess. On Hygeia's shrine
Obsequious Gnomes repose the lyre divine;
Descending Sylphs relax the trembling strings,
And catch the rain-drops on their shadowy wings.

And now her vase a modest Naiad fills
With liquid crystal from her pebbly rills;
Piles the dry cedar round her silver urn
(Bright climbs the blaze, the crackling faggots burn),
Culls the green herb of China's envied bowers;
In gaudy cups the steaming treasure pours;
And, sweetly smiling, on her bended knee
Presents the fragrant quintessence of Tea.

End of Canto Two

Canto Three

And now the Goddess sounds her silver shell
And shakes with deeper tones the enchanted dell.
Pale round her grassy throne, bedew'd with tears,
Flit the thin forms of Sorrows and of Fears;
Soft Sighs responsive whisper to the chords,
And Indignations half-unsheathe their swords.

" Thrice round the grave Circaea[63] prints her tread,
And chants the numbers which disturb the dead;
Shakes o'er the holy earth her sable plume,
Waves her dread wand, and strikes the echoing tomb!
Pale shoot the stars across the troubled night;
The tim'rous moon withholds her conscious light;
Shrill scream the famish'd bats and shivering owls,
And loud and long the dog of midnight howls!
Then yawns the bursting ground! *Two* imps obscene
Rise on broad wings and hail the baleful queen:
Each with dire grin salutes the potent wand,
And leads the sorceress with his sooty hand.
Onward they glide where sheds the sickly yew
O'er many a mouldering bone its nightly dew;
The ponderous portals of the church unbar
(Hoarse on their hinge the ponderous portals jar).
As through the colour'd glass the moon-beam falls,
Huge shapeless spectres quiver on the walls;
Low murmurs creep along the hollow ground,
And to each step the pealing aisles resound.
By glimmering lamps, protecting saints among
(The shrines all trembling as they pass along),
O'er the still choir with hideous laugh they move;
Fiends yell below, and angels weep above.
Their impious march to God's high altar bend;
With feet impure the sacred steps ascend;
With wine unbless'd the holy chalice stain,
Assume the mitre, and the cope profane.
To heaven their eyes in mock devotion throw,
And to the cross with horrid mummery[64] bow;
Adjure by mimic rites the powers above,
And plight, alternate, their Satanic love.

---

[63] enchanter's nightshade
[64] buffoonery [JD]

" Avaunt ye vulgar! from her sacred groves
With maniac step the Pythian Laura[65] moves.
Full of the god her labouring bosom sighs,
Foam on her lips, and fury in her eyes;
Strong writhe her limbs; her wild dishevell'd hair
Starts from her laurel-wreath and swims in air.
While *twenty* priests the gorgeous shrine surround,
Cinctured with ephods[66], and with garlands crown'd,
Contending hosts and trembling nations wait
The firm immutable behests of Fate.
She speaks in thunder from her golden throne
With words unwill'd, and wisdom not her own.

" So on his Night-Mare, through the evening fog,
Flits the squab Fiend o'er fen, and lake, and bog;
Seeks some love-wilder'd maid with sleep oppress'd;
Alights, and grinning sits upon her breast.
Such as of late amid the murky sky
Was mark'd by Fuseli's poetic eye,
Whose daring tints, with Shakespeare's happiest grace,
Gave to the airy phantom form and place.
Back o'er her pillow sinks her blushing head;
Her snow-white limbs hang helpless from the bed,
While with quick sighs and suffocative breath,
Her interrupted heart-pulse swims in death.
Then shrieks of captured towns, and widows' tears,
Pale lovers stretched upon their blood-stain'd biers,
The headlong precipice that thwarts her flight,
The trackless desert, the cold starless night,
And stern-eyed murderer with his knife behind,
In dread succession agonize her mind.
O'er her fair limbs convulsive tremors fleet,
Start in her hands, and struggle in her feet.
In vain to scream with quivering lips she tries,
And strains in palsy'd lids her tremulous eyes.
In vain she *wills* to run, fly, swim, walk, creep:
The Will presides not in the bower of Sleep.
On her fair bosom sits the Demon-Ape
Erect, and balances his bloated shape;
Rolls in their marble orbs his Gorgon-eyes,
And drinks with leathern ears her tender cries.

---

65 i.e. laurel [ed.]
66 dressed in sashes and surplices [ed.]

" Arm'd with her ivory beak and talon-hands,
Descending Fica[67] dives into the sands;
Chamber'd in earth with cold oblivion lies,
Nor heeds, ye suitor-train, your amorous sighs;
Erewhile with renovated beauty blooms,
Mounts into air,and moves her leafy plumes.

" Where Hamps and Manifold, their cliffs among,
Each in his flinty channel winds along,
With lucid lines the dusky moor divides,
Hurrying to intermix their sister tides;
Where still their silver-bosom'd Nymphs abhor
The blood-smear'd mansion of gigantic Thor[68];
Erst, fires volcanic in the marble womb
Of cloud-wrapp'd Wetton raised the massy dome;
Rocks rear'd on rocks in huge disjointed piles
Form the tall turrets and the lengthen'd aisles;
Broad ponderous piers sustain the roof, and wide
Branch the vast rainbow ribs from side to side;
While from above descends in milky streams
One scanty pencil of illusive beams,
Suspended crags and gaping gulfs illumes,
And gilds the horrors of the deepen'd glooms.

" Here oft the Naiads, as they chanced to stray
Near the dread fane on Thor's returning day,
Saw from red altars streams of guiltless blood
Stain their green reed-beds, and pollute their flood;
Heard dying babes in wicker prisons wail,
And shrieks of matrons thrill the affrighted gale;
While from dark caves infernal echoes mock,
And fiends triumphant shout from every rock!

" So, still the Nymphs emerging lift in air
Their snow-white shoulders and their azure hair;
Sail with sweet grace the dimpling streams along,
Listening the shepherd's or the miner's song;
But when afar they view the giant cave,
On timorous fins they circle on the wave,
With streaming eyes and throbbing hearts recoil,
Plunge their fair forms, and dive beneath the soil.

---

67 Indian fig
68 Thor's Cave in the Manifold valley near Wetton, Staffordshire. The Manifold dives underground near Thor's Cave (totally in dry weather). The rivers Hamps and Manifold run underground for three miles before resurfacing at Ilam. In wet weather both run overground too. [ed.]

Closed round their heads reluctant eddies sink,
And wider rings successive dash the brink.
Three thousand steps in sparry clefts they stray,
Or seek through sullen mines their gloomy way;
On beds of lava sleep in coral cells,
Or sigh o'er jasper fish and agate shells.
Till, where famed Ilam leads his boiling floods
Through flowery meadows and impending woods,
Pleased, with light spring they leave the dreary night,
And 'mid circumfluent surges rise to light;
Shake their bright locks, the widening vale pursue,
Their sea-green mantles fringed with pearly dew.
In playful groups by towering Thorp they move,
Bound o'er the foaming weirs, and rush into the Dove.

" With fierce distracted eye Impatiens[69] stands,
Swells her pale cheeks, and brandishes her hands;
With rage and hate the astonish'd groves alarms,
And hurls her infants from her frantic arms.

" So when Medea left her native soil,
Unawed by danger, unsubdued by toil,
Her weeping sire and beckoning friends withstood,
And launch'd enamour'd on the boiling flood;
One ruddy boy her gentle lips caress'd,
And one fair girl was pillow'd on her breast;
While high in air the golden treasure burns,
And Love and Glory guide the prow by turns.
But, when Thessalia's inauspicious plain
Received the matron-heroine from the main,
While horns of triumph sound, and altars burn,
And shouting nations hail their chief's return,
Aghast, she saw new-deck'd the nuptial bed,
And proud Creusa to the temple led;
Saw her in Jason's mercenary arms
Deride her virtues, and insult her charms;
Saw her dear babes from fame and empire torn,
In foreign realms deserted and forlorn;
Her love rejected, and her vengeance braved,
By him her beauties won, her virtues saved.
With stern regard she eyed the traitor-king,
And felt, Ingratitude! thy keenest sting.
'Nor Heaven,' she cried, 'nor Earth, nor Hell can hold
A heart abandon'd to the thirst of gold!'

---

69 touch-me-not, (named 'Impatiens noli-tangere' by Linnaeus [ed.])

Stamp'd with wild foot, and shook her horrent brow,
And call'd the Furies from their dens below.
Slow out of earth, before the festive crowds,
On wheels of fire, amid a night of clouds,
Drawn by fierce fiends arose a magic car,
Received the Queen, and hovering flamed in air.
As with raised hands the suppliant traitors kneel,
And fear the vengeance they deserve to feel,
Thrice with parch'd lips her guiltless babes she press'd,
And thrice she clasp'd them to her tortured breast;
Awhile with white uplifted eyes she stood,
Then plung'd her trembling poniard[70] in their blood.
'Go, kiss your sire! go, share the bridal mirth!'
She cried, and hurl'd their quivering limbs on earth.
Rebellowing thunders rock the marble towers,
And red-tongued lightnings shoot their arrowy showers.
Earth yawns! The crashing ruin sinks. O'er all,
Death with black hands extends his mighty pall.
Their mingling gore the Fiends of Vengeance quaff,
And Hell receives them with convulsive laugh.

" Round the vex'd isles where fierce tornadoes roar,
Or tropic breezes soothe the sultry shore;
What time the eve her gauze pellucid spreads
O'er the dim flowers, and veils the misty meads;
Slow o'er the twilight sands or leafy walks,
With gloomy dignity Dictamna[71] stalks;
In sulphurous eddies round the weird dame
Plays the light gas, or kindles into flame.
If rests the traveller his weary head,
Grim Mancinella[72] haunts the mossy bed,
Brews her black hebenon[73], and, stealing near,
Pours the curs'd venom in his tortured ear.
Wide o'er the madd'ning throng Urtica[74] flings
Her barbed shafts, and darts her poison'd stings.
And fell Lobelia's[75] suffocating breath
Loads the dank pinion of the gale with death.
With fear and hate they blast the affrighted groves,
Yet own with tender care their kindred Loves!

---

[70] small pointed dagger [JD]
[71] Fraxinella (burning bush [ed.])
[72] Hippomane
[73] poisonous juice [ed.]
[74] nettle
[75] Lobelia longiflora (West Indies)

"So, where Palmyra 'mid her wasted plains,
Her shatter'd aqueducts and prostrate fanes,
(As the bright orb of breezy midnight pours
Long threads of silver through her gaping towers,
O'er mouldering tombs and tottering columns gleams,
And frosts her deserts with diffusive beams),
Sad o'er the mighty wreck in silence bends,
Lifts her wet eyes, her tremulous hands extends.
If from lone cliffs a bursting rill expands
Its transient course, and sinks into the sands,
O'er the moist rock the fell hyena prowls,
The leopard hisses, and the panther growls;
On quivering wing the famish'd vulture screams,
Dips his dry beak and sweeps the gushing streams;
With foaming jaws beneath, and sanguine tongue,
Laps the lean wolf, and pants, and runs along;
Stern stalks the lion, on the rustling brinks
Hears the dread snake, and trembles as he drinks;
Quick darts the scaly monster o'er the plain,
Fold after fold, his undulating train;
And bending o'er the lake his crested brow,
Starts at the crocodile that gapes below.

"Where seas of glass with gay reflections smile
Round the green coasts of Java's palmy isle,
A spacious plain extends its upland scene:
Rocks rise on rocks, and fountains gush between;
Soft zephyrs blow, eternal summers reign,
And showers prolific bless the soil - in vain!
No spicy nutmeg scents the vernal gales,
Nor towering plantain shades the mid-day vales;
No grassy mantle hides the sable hills,
No flowery chaplet crowns the trickling rills;
Nor tufted moss, nor leathery lichen creeps
In russet tapestry o'er the crumbling steeps.
No step retreating, on the sand impress'd,
Invites the visit of a second guest;
No refluent fin the unpeopled stream divides,
No revolant pinion cleaves the airy tides;
Nor handed moles, nor beaked worms return,
That, mining, pass the irremeable bourn[76].
Fierce in dread silence on the blasted heath
Fell Upas[77] sits, the Hydra-Tree of death.

---

[76] a boundary admitting no return
[77] Bohon-Upas (Malay). Mythical poisonous tentacular 'tree of death' [ed.]

Lo, from one root, the envenom'd soil below,
A thousand vegetative serpents grow;
In shining rays the scaly monster spreads
O'er ten square leagues his far-diverging heads;
Or in one trunk entwists his tangled form,
Looks o'er the clouds, and hisses in the storm.
Steep'd in fell poison, as his sharp teeth part,
A thousand tongues in quick vibration dart;
Snatch the proud eagle towering o'er the heath,
Or pounce the lion as he stalks beneath;
Or strew, as marshall'd hosts contend in vain,
With human skeletons the whiten'd plain.
Chain'd at his root two scion-demons dwell,
Breathe the faint hiss, or try the shriller yell;
Rise, fluttering in the air on callow wings,
And aim at insect-prey their little stings.
So Time's strong arms with sweeping scythe erase
Art's cumbrous works, and empires, from their base;
While each young Hour its sickle fine employs,
And crops the sweet buds of domestic joys!

" With blushes bright as morn fair Orchis charms,
And lulls her infant in her fondling arms;
Soft plays Affection round her bosom's throne,
And guards his life, forgetful of her own.
So wings the wounded deer her headlong flight,
Pierced by some ambush'd archer of the night,
Shoots to the woodlands with her bounding fawn,
And drops of blood bedew the conscious lawn.
There hid in shades she shuns the cheerful day,
Hangs o'er her young, and weeps her life away.

" So stood Eliza on the wood-crown'd height
O'er Minden's plain, spectatress of the fight;
Sought with bold eye amid the bloody strife
Her dearer self, the partner of her life;
From hill to hill the rushing host pursued,
And view'd his banner, or believed she view'd.
Pleased with the distant roar, with quicker tread
Fast by his hand one lisping boy she led,
And one fair girl amid the loud alarm
Slept on her kerchief, cradled by her arm,
While round her brows bright beams of honour dart,
And love's warm eddies circle round her heart.
Near and more near the intrepid beauty press'd,
Saw through the driving smoke his dancing crest;

Saw on his helm (her virgin-hands inwove)
Bright stars of gold, and mystic knots of love;
Heard the exulting shout, 'They run! they run!'.
'Great God!' she cried, 'he's safe; the battle's won!'
A ball now hisses through the airy tides,
(Some Fury wing'd it, and some demon guides!)
Parts the fine locks her graceful head that deck,
Wounds her fair ear, and sinks into her neck.
The red stream, issuing from her azure veins,
Dyes her white veil, her ivory bosom stains.
'Ah me!' she cried, and sinking on the ground
Kiss'd her dear babes, regardless of the wound.
'Oh, cease not yet to beat, thou vital urn!
Wait, gushing life, oh, wait my love's return!
Hoarse barks the wolf, the vulture screams from far.
The angel, Pity, shuns the walks of war.
Oh spare, ye war-hounds, spare their tender age!
On me, on me,' she cried, 'exhaust your rage!'
Then with weak arms her weeping babes caress'd
And, sighing, hid them in her blood-stain'd vest.
From tent to tent the impatient warrior flies,
Fear in his heart, and frenzy in his eyes;
Eliza's name along the camp he calls;
'Eliza' echoes through the canvas walls.
Quick through the murmuring gloom his footsteps tread
O'er groaning heaps (the dying and the dead),
Vault o'er the plain, and in the tangled wood.
Lo! dead Eliza, weltering in her blood!
Soon hears his listening son the welcome sounds;
With open arms and sparkling eyes he bounds.
'Speak low,' he cries, and gives his little hand,
'Eliza sleeps upon the dew-cold sand.'
Poor weeping babe with bloody fingers press'd,
And tried with pouting lips her milkless breast.
'Alas! we both with cold and hunger quake.
Why do you weep? Mama will soon awake.'
'She'll wake no more!' the hopeless mourner cried,
Upturn'd his eyes, and clasp'd his hands, and sigh'd.
Stretch'd on the ground awhile entranced he lay,
And press'd warm kisses on the lifeless clay;
And then upsprung with wild convulsive start,
And all the father kindled in his heart.
'Oh, Heavens!' he cried, 'my first rash vow forgive;
These bind to Earth, for these I pray to live!'
Round his chill babes he wrapp'd his crimson vest,
And clasp'd them sobbing to his aching breast.

"*Two* harlot-nymphs, the fair Cuscutas[78], please
With labour'd negligence, and studied ease;
In the meek garb of modest worth disguised,
The eye averted, and the smile chastised,
With sly approach they spread their dangerous charms,
And round their victim wind their wiry arms.
So by Scamander when Laocoon stood,
Where Troy's proud turrets glitter'd in the flood,
Raised high his arm, and with prophetic call
To shrinking realms announced her fated fall;
Whirled his fierce spear with more than mortal force,
And pierced the thick ribs of the echoing horse.
Two serpent-forms incumbent on the main,
Lashing the white waves with redundant train,
Arch'd their blue necks, and shook their towering crests,
And plough'd their foamy way with speckled breasts;
Then, darting fierce amid the affrighted throngs,
Roll'd their red eyes, and shot their forked tongues.
Two daring youths to guard the hoary sire
Thwart their dread progress, and provoke their ire.
Round sire and sons the scaly monsters roll'd,
Ring above ring, in many a tangled fold,
Close and more close their writhing limbs surround,
And fix with foamy teeth the envenom'd wound.
With brow upturn'd to heaven the holy sage
In silent agony sustains their rage;
While each fond youth, in vain, with piercing cries
Bends on the tortured sire his dying eyes.

" 'Drink deep, sweet youths,' seductive Vitis cries,
The maudlin tear-drop glittering in her eyes;
Green leaves and purple clusters crown her head,
And the tall Thyrsus[79] stays her tottering tread.
Five hapless swains with soft assuasive smiles
The harlot meshes in her deathful toils.
'Drink deep,' she carols, as she waves in air
The mantling goblet, 'and forget your care.'
O'er the dread feast malignant Chemia scowls,
And mingles poison in the nectar'd bowls;
Fell Gout peeps grinning through the flimsy scene,
And bloated Dropsy pants behind unseen;

---

78 dodder (a parasitic creeper [ed.])
79 wand usually carried by Dionysus [ed.]

Wrapp'd in his robe white Lepra hides his stains,
And silent Frenzy, writhing, bites his chains.

" So when Prometheus braved the Thunderer's ire,
Stole from his blazing throne ethereal fire,
And lantern'd in his breast, from realms of day
Bore the bright treasure to his Man of clay;
High on cold Caucasus by Vulcan bound,
The lean impatient vulture fluttering round,
His writhing limbs in vain he twists and strains
To break or loose the adamantine chains.
The gluttonous bird, exulting in his pangs,
Tears his swoll'n liver with remorseless fangs.

" The gentle Cyclamen with dewy eye
Breathes o'er her lifeless babe the parting sigh;
And, bending low to earth, with pious hands
Inhumes her dear departed in the sands.
'Sweet Nursling! withering in thy tender hour,
Oh, sleep,' she cries, 'and rise a fairer flower!'
So when the plague o'er London's gasping crowds
Shook her dank wing, and steer'd her murky clouds;
When o'er the friendless bier no rites were read,
No dirge slow-chanted, and no pall outspread;
While Death and Night piled up the naked throng,
And Silence drove their ebon cars along;
Six lovely daughters, and their father, swept
To the throng'd grave. Cleone saw, and wept.
Her tender mind, with meek religion fraught,
Drank, all-resign'd, Affliction's bitter draught,
Alive and listening to the whisper'd groan
Of others' woes, unconscious of her own.
One smiling boy, her last sweet hope, she warms,
Hush'd, on her bosom, circled in her arms.
Daughter of Woe! ere morn, in vain caress'd,
Clung the cold babe upon thy milkless breast;
With feeble cries thy last sad aid required,
Stretch'd its stiff limbs and on thy lap expired.
Long with wide eyelids on her child she gazed,
And long to Heaven their tearless orbs she raised;
Then with quick foot and throbbing heart she found
Where Chartreuse open'd deep his holy ground;
Bore her last treasure through the midnight gloom,
And kneeling dropp'd it in the mighty tomb.
'I follow next!' the frantic mourner said,
And living plunged amid the festering dead.

"Where vast Ontario rolls his brineless tides,
And feeds the trackless forests on his sides,
Fair Cassia trembling hears the howling woods,
And trusts her tawny children to the floods.
Cinctured with gold while *ten* fond brothers stand,
And guard the beauty on her native land,
Soft breathes the gale, the current gently moves,
And bears to Norway's coasts her infant-loves.
So the sad mother at the noon of night
From bloody Memphis stole her silent flight;
Wrapp'd her dear babe beneath her folded vest,
And clasp'd the treasure to her throbbing breast;
With soothing whispers hush'd its feeble cry,
Press'd the soft kiss, and breathed the secret sigh.
With dauntless step she seeks the winding shore,
Hears unappall'd the glimmering torrents roar;
With paper-flags a floating cradle weaves,
And hides the smiling boy in Lotus-leaves;
Gives her white bosom to his eager lips,
The salt-tears mingling with the milk he sips;
Waits on the reed-crown'd brink with pious guile,
And trusts the scaly monsters of the Nile.
Erewhile, majestic from his lone abode,
Ambassador of Heaven, the Prophet trod;
Wrench'd the red scourge from proud Oppression's hands,
And broke, curs'd Slavery, thy iron bands.

"Hark! heard ye not that piercing cry,
Which shook the waves and rent the sky?
E'en now, e'en now on yonder western shores
Weeps pale Despair, and writhing Anguish roars;
E'en now in Afric's groves, with hideous yell
Fierce Slavery stalks, and slips the dogs of hell;
From vale to vale the gathering cries rebound,
And sable nations tremble at the sound!
Ye bands of Senators! whose suffrage sways
Britannia's realms, whom either Ind obeys;
Who right the injured and reward the brave,
Stretch your strong arm, for ye have power to save!
Throned in the vaulted heart, his dread resort,
Inexorable Conscience holds his court;
With still small voice the plots of Guilt alarms,
Bares his mask'd brow, his lifted hand disarms;
But, wrapp'd in night, with terrors all his own,
He speaks in thunder, when the deed is done.

Hear him, ye Senates! hear this truth sublime,
'He who allows oppression shares the crime.'

" No radiant pearl which crested Fortune wears,
No gem that twinkling hangs from Beauty's ears,
Not the bright stars which night's blue arch adorn,
Nor rising suns that gild the vernal morn,
Shine with such lustre as the tear that flows
Down Virtue's manly cheek for others' woes."[80]

Here ceased the Muse, and dropp'd her tuneful shell;
Tumultuous woes her panting bosom swell.
O'er her flush'd cheek her gauzy veil she throws,
Folds her white arms and bends her laurell'd brows.
For human guilt awhile the Goddess sighs,
And human sorrows dim celestial eyes.

End of Canto Three

80 This couplet is the version found in the 1824 edition. [ed.]

Canto Four

Now the broad sun his golden orb unshrouds,
Flames in the west, and paints the parted clouds.
O'er heaven's wide arch refracted lustres flow,
And bend in air the many-colour'd bow.
The tuneful Goddess on the glowing sky
Fix'd in mute ecstasy her glistening eye;
And then her lute to sweeter tones she strung,
And swell'd with softer chords the Paphian[81] song.
Long aisles of oak return'd the silver sound,
And amorous Echoes talk'd along the ground.
Pleased Lichfield listen'd from her sacred bowers,
Bow'd her tall groves, and shook her stately towers.

" Nymph! not for thee the radiant day returns,
Nymph! not for thee the golden solstice burns,
Refulgent Cerea![82] At the dusky hour
She seeks with pensive step the mountain-bower,
Bright as the blush of rising morn, and warms
The dull cold eye of Midnight with her charms.
There to the skies she lifts her pencill'd brows,
Opes her fair lips, and breathes her virgin vows;
Eyes the white zenith; counts the suns that roll
Their distant fires, and blaze around the Pole;
Or marks where Jove directs his glittering car
O'er heaven's blue vault: herself a brighter star.
There as soft zephyrs sweep with pausing airs
Thy snowy neck, and part thy shadowy hairs,
Sweet maid of night! to Cynthia's sober beams
Glows thy warm cheek, thy polish'd bosom gleams.
In crowds around thee gaze the admiring swains,
And guard in silence the enchanted plains;
Drop the still tear, or breathe the impassion'd sigh,
And drink inebriate rapture from thine eye.
Thus when old Needwood's hoary scenes the night
Paints with blue shadow, and with milky light;
Where Mundy pour'd, the listening nymphs among,
Loud to the echoing vales his parting song;
With measur'd step the Fairy-Sovereign treads,
Shakes her high plume, and glitters o'er the meads;
Round each green holly leads her sportive train,
And little footsteps mark the circled plain.

---

81 i.e. belonging to Venus and her temple at Paphos [ed.]
82 the night-blooming Cereus

**Each haunted rill with silver voices rings,
And night's sweet bird in livelier accents sings.**

**" Ere the bright star, which leads the morning sky,
Hangs o'er the blushing east his diamond-eye,
The chaste Tropaeo[83] leaves her secret bed
(A saint-like glory trembles round her head).
Eight watchful swains along the lawns of night
With amorous steps pursue the virgin-light;
O'er her fair form the electric lustre plays,
And cold she moves amid the lambent blaze.
So shines the glow-fly, when the sun retires,
And gems the night air with phosphoric fires.
Thus o'er the marsh aerial lights betray,
And charm the unwary wanderer from his way.
So when thy king, Assyria, fierce and proud,
Three human victims to his idol vow'd;
Rear'd a vast pyre before the golden shrine
Of sulphurous coal, and pitch-exuding pine.
Loud roar the flames, the iron nostrils breathe,
And the huge bellows pant and heave beneath;
Bright, and more bright, the blazing deluge flows,
And white with sevenfold heat the furnace glows.
And now the Monarch fix'd with dread surprise
Deep in the burning vault his dazzled eyes.
'Lo! three, unbound, amid the frightful glare,
Unscorch'd their sandals, and unsing'd their hair.
And now a fourth, with seraph-beauty bright
Descends, accosts them, and outshines the light.
Fierce flames, innocuous, as they step, retire;
And slow they move amid a world of fire!'
He spoke; to Heaven his arms repentant spread,
And kneeling bow'd his gem-incircled head.**

**" *Two* sister-nymphs, the fair Avenas[84], lead
Their fleecy squadrons on the lawns of Tweed;
Pass with light step his wave-worn banks along,
And wake his echoes with their silver tongue;
Or touch the reed, as gentle Love inspires,
In notes accordant to their chaste desires.**

---

83 Trapaeolum majus, Indian cress
84 Avena, oat

1

'Sweet Echo! sleeps thy vocal shell,
Where this high arch o'erhangs the dell;
While Tweed with sun-reflecting streams
Chequers thy rocks with dancing beams?

2

Here may no clamours harsh intrude,
No brawling hound or clarion rude;
Here no fell beast of midnight prowl,
And teach thy tortured cliffs to howl!

3

Be thine to pour these vales along
Some artless shepherd's evening song;
While night's sweet bird, from yon high spray
Responsive, listens to his lay.

4

And if, like me, some love-lorn maid
Should sing her sorrows to thy shade,
Oh, soothe her breast, ye rocks around!
With softest sympathy of sound.'

" From ozier boughs the brooding halcyons peep,
The swans pursuing cleave the glassy deep,
On hovering wings the wondering reed-larks play,
And silent bitterns listen to the lay.
Three shepherd-swains beneath the beechen shades
Twine rival garlands for the tuneful maids;
On each smooth bark the mystic love-knot frame,
Or on white sands inscribe the favour'd name.
Green swells the beech, the widening knots improve,
So spread the tender growths of living love;
Wave follows wave, the letter'd lines decay,
So Love's soft forms uncultured melt away.

" From time's remotest dawn, where China brings
In proud succession all her patriot-kings;
O'er desert-sands, deep gulfs, and hills sublime,
Extends her massy Wall from clime to clime.

With bells and dragons crests her pagod-bowers,
Her silken palaces, and porcelain towers;
With long canals a thousand nations laves;
Plants all her wilds, and peoples all her waves.
Slow treads fair Cannabis[85] the breezy strand
(The distaff streams dishevell'd in her hand);
Now to the left her ivory neck inclines,
And leads in Paphian[86] curves its azure lines;
Dark waves the fringed lid, the warm cheek glows,
And the fair ear the parting locks disclose;
Now to the right with airy sweep she bends,
Quick join the threads, the dancing spole depends.
***Five* swains, attracted, guard the Nymph by turns;**
Her grace inchants them, and her beauty burns;
To each she bows with sweet assuasive smile,
Hears his soft vows, and turns her spole the while.
So, when with light and shade (concordant strife!)
Stern Clotho weaves the chequer'd thread of life,
Hour after hour the growing line extends;
The cradle and the coffin bound its ends.
Soft cords of silk the whirling spoles reveal,
If smiling Fortune turn the giddy wheel;
But if sweet Love, with baby-fingers, twines
And wets with dewy lips the lengthening lines,
Skein after skein celestial tints unfold,
And all the silken tissue shines with gold.

" Warm with sweet blushes bright Galantha[87] glows,
And prints with frolic step the melting snows;
O'er silent floods, white hills, and glittering meads,
***Six* rival swains the playful beauty leads;**
Chides with her dulcet voice the tardy Spring;
Bids slumbering Zephyr stretch his folded wing;
Wakes the hoarse cuckoo in his gloomy cave,
And calls the wondering dormouse from his grave;
Bids the mute redbreast cheer the budding grove,
And plaintive ringdove tune her notes to love.

" Spring! with thy own sweet smile and tuneful tongue,
Delighted Bellis[88] calls her infant throng.

---

[85] Chinese hemp
[86] William Hogarth's serpentine 'line of beauty', associated with Venus at Paphos [ed.]
[87] Galanthus nivalis, snowdrop
[88] Bellis prolifera, hen-and-chicken daisy

**Each on his reed astride, the cherub-train
Watch her kind looks, and circle o'er the plain;
Now with young wonder touch the sliding snail,
Admire his eye-tipp'd horns, and painted mail;
Chase with quick step and eager arms outspread,
The pausing butterfly from mead to mead;
Or twine green oziers with the fragrant Gale[89],
The azure harebell, and the primrose pale;
Join hand in hand, and in procession gay
Adorn with votive wreaths the shrine of May.
So moves the Goddess to the Idalian groves,
And leads her gold-hair'd family of Loves.
These, from the flaming furnace, strong and bold,
Pour the red steel in many a sandy mould;
On tinkling anvils (with Vulcanian art)
Turn with hot tongs, and forge the dreadful dart;
The barbed head on whirling jaspers grind,
And dip the point in poison for the mind;
Each polish'd shaft with snow-white plumage wing,
Or strain the bow reluctant to its string.
These on light pinion twine with busy hands,
Or stretch from bough to bough the flowery bands;
Scare the dark beetle as he wheels on high,
Or catch in silken nets the gilded fly;
Call the young Zephyrs to their fragrant bowers,
And stay with kisses sweet the Vernal Hours.**

**" Where, as proud Masson rises rude and bleak,
And with misshapen turrets crests the Peak,
Old Matlock gapes with marble jaws beneath,
And o'er scared Derwent bends his flinty teeth;
Deep in wide caves below the dangerous soil,
Blue sulphurs flame, imprison'd waters boil;
Impetuous steams in spiral columns rise
Through rifted rocks, impatient for the skies;
Or o'er bright seas of bubbling lavas blow,
As heave and toss the billowy fires below;
Condensed on high, in wandering rills they glide
From Masson's dome, and burst his sparry side;
Round his grey towers, and down his fringed walls,
From cliff to cliff the liquid treasure falls;
In beds of stalactite, bright ores among,
O'er corals, shells, and crystals, winds along;**

[89] Myrica gale, myrtle

Crusts the green mosses and the tangled wood,
And sparkling plunges to its parent flood.
O'er the warm wave a smiling youth presides,
Attunes its murmurs, its meanders guides;
The blooming Fucus[90], in her sparry coves,
To amorous Echo sings his *secret* loves;
Bathes his fair forehead in the misty stream,
And with sweet breath perfumes the rising steam.
So, erst, an Angel o'er Bethesda's springs,
Each morn descending, shook his dewy wings;
And as his bright translucent form he laves,
Salubrious powers enrich the troubled waves.

" Amphibious nymph from Nile's prolific bed,
Emerging Trapa[91] lifts her pearly head;
Fair glows her virgin cheek and modest breast,
A panoply of scales deforms the rest;
Her quivering fins and panting gills she hides,
But spreads her silver arms upon the tides;
Slow as she sails, her ivory neck she laves,
And shakes her golden tresses o'er the waves.
Charm'd round the Nymph, in circling gambols glide
***Four* Nereid-forms, or shoot along the tide;**
Now all as one they rise with frolic spring,
And beat the wondering air on humid wing;
Now all descending plunge beneath the main,
And lash the foam with undulating train;
Above, below, they wheel, retreat, advance,
In air and ocean weave the mazy dance;
Bow their quick heads , and point their diamond-eyes,
And twinkle to the sun with ever-changing dyes.

" Where Andes, crested with volcanic beams,
Sheds a long line of light on Plata's streams;
Opes all his springs, unlocks his golden caves,
And feeds and freights the immeasurable waves;
Delighted Ocyma[92] at twilight hours
Calls her light car, and leaves the sultry bowers;
Love's rising ray, and youth's seductive dye,
Bloom'd on her cheek, and brighten'd in her eye;
Chaste, pure, and white, a zone of silver graced
Her tender breast, as white, as pure, as chaste;

---

90 a fresh water alga [ed.]
91 Trapa natans, water chestnut [ed.]
92 Ocymum salinum, saline basil

By *four* fond swains in playful circles drawn,
On glowing wheels she tracks the moon-bright lawn,
Mounts the rude cliff, unveils her blushing charms,
And calls the panting Zephyrs to her arms.
Emerged from ocean springs the vaporous air,
Bathes her light limbs, uncurls her amber hair,
Incrusts her beamy form with films saline,
And beauty blazes through the crystal shrine.
So with pellucid studs the ice-flower[93] gems
Her rimy foliage and her candied stems.
So from his glassy horns and pearly eyes,
The diamond-beetle darts a thousand dyes;
Mounts with enamell'd wings the vesper gale,
And wheeling shines in adamantine mail.

" Thus when loud thunders o'er Gomorrah burst,
And heaving earthquakes shook his realms accurst,
An angel-guest led forth the trembling Fair,
With shadowy hand, and warn'd the guiltless pair:
'Haste from these lands of sin, ye righteous, fly!
Speed the quick step, nor turn the lingering eye!'
Such the command, as fabling bards recite,
When Orpheus charm'd the grisly king of night;
Sooth'd the pale phantoms with his plaintive lay,
And led the fair assurgent into day.
Wide yawn'd the earth, the fiery tempest flash'd,
And towns and towers in on vast ruin crash'd;
Onward they move; loud horror roars behind,
And shrieks of anguish bellow in the wind.
With many a sob, amid a thousand fears,
The beauteous wanderer pours her gushing tears;
Each soft connection rends her troubled breast:
She turns, unconscious of the stern behest!
'I faint! I fall! ah, me! sensations chill
Shoot through my bones, my shuddering bosom thrill!
I freeze! I freeze! just Heaven regards my fault,
Numbs my cold limbs, and hardens into salt.
Not yet, not yet, your dying Love resign!
This last, last kiss receive! no longer thine!'
She said, and ceased. Her stiffen'd form he press'd,
And strain'd the briny column to his breast;
Printed with quivering lips the lifeless snow,
And wept, and gazed, the monument of woe.

---

93 Mesembryanthemum crystallinum

So when Aeneas through the flames of Troy
Bore his pale sire, and led his lovely boy;
With loitering step the fair Creusa stay'd,
And death involved her in eternal shade.
Oft the lone pilgrim, that his road forsakes,
Marks the wide ruins, and the sulphur'd lakes;
On mouldering piles amid asphaltic mud
Hears the hoarse bittern where Gomorrah stood;
Recalls the unhappy Pair with lifted eye,
Leans on the crystal tomb, and breathes the silent sigh.

" With net-wove sash and glittering gorget dress'd,
And scarlet robe lapell'd upon her breast,
Stern Ara[94] frowns, the measured march assumes,
Trails her long lance, and nods her shadowy plumes;
While Love's soft beams illume her treacherous eyes,
And Beauty lightens through the thin disguise.
So erst, when Hercules, untamed by toil,
Own'd the soft power of Dejanira's smile,
His lion-spoils the laughing Fair demands,
And gives the distaff to his awkward hands;
O'er her white neck the bristly mane she throws,
And binds the gaping whiskers on her brows;
Plaits round her slender waist the shaggy vest,
And clasps the velvet paws across her breast.
Next with soft hands the knotted club she rears,
Heaves up from earth, and on her shoulder bears.
Onward with loftier step the Beauty treads,
And trails the brinded ermine o'er the meads;
Wolves, bears and pards forsake the affrighted groves,
And grinning Satyrs tremble, as she moves.

" Caryo's sweet smile Dianthus proud admires,[95]
And gazing burns with unallow'd desires;
With sighs and sorrows her compassion moves,
And wins the damsel to illicit loves.
The monster-offspring heirs the father's pride,
Mask'd in the damask beauties of the bride.
So when the nightingale in eastern bowers
On quivering pinion woos the queen of flowers;
Inhales her fragrance, as he hangs in air,
And melts with melody the blushing fair;

94 Arum maculatum, cuckoo pint
95 There is a kind of pink called Fairchild's mule which is here supposed to be produced between a Dianthus superbus and the Caryophillus, clove.

Half-rose, half-bird, a beauteous monster springs,
Waves his thin leaves, and claps his glossy wings;
Long horrent thorns his mossy legs surround,
And tendril-talons root him to the ground;
Green films of rind his wrinkled neck o'erspread,
And crimson petals crest his curled head;
Soft warbling beaks in each bright blossom move,
And vocal rosebuds thrill the enchanted grove!
Admiring Evening stays her beamy star,
And still Night listens from his ebon car,
While on white wings descending Houris[96] throng,
And drink the floods of odour and of song.

" When from his golden urn the Solstice pours
O'er Afric's sable sons the sultry hours;
When not a gale flits o'er her tawny hills,
Save where the dry Harmattan breathes and kills;
When stretch'd in dust her gasping panthers lie,
And writhed in foamy folds her serpents die;
Indignant Atlas mourns his leafless woods,
And Gambia trembles for his sinking floods;
Contagion stalks along the briny sand,
And Ocean rolls his sick'ning shoals to land.
Fair Chunda[97] smiles amid the burning waste,
Her brow unturban'd, and her zone unbraced;
***Ten* brother-youths with light umbrellas shade,**
Or fan with busy hands the panting maid;
Loose wave her locks, disclosing, as they break,
The rising bosom and averted cheek;
Clasp'd round her ivory neck with studs of gold
Flows her thin vest in many a gauzy fold;
O'er her light limbs the dim transparence plays,
And the fair form it seems to hide, betrays.

[" Cold from a thousand rocks, where Ganges leads (i)[98]
The gushing waters to his sultry meads;
By moon-crown'd mosques with gay reflections glides,
And vast pagodas trembling on his sides;
With sweet loquacity Nelumbo[99] sails, (v)
Shouts to his shores, and parleys with his gales;

---

96 damsels of the Muslim paradise [ed.]
97 Hedysarum gyrans
98 These 18 lines first appear in the fourth edition of 1794 [ed.]
99 Nymphaea nelumbo; the capsule is perforated with holes at the top, and the seeds rattle in it.

Invokes his echoes, as she moves along,
And thrills his rippling surges with her song.
As round the Nymph her listening lovers play,
And guard the Beauty on her watery way;
Charm'd on the brink relenting tigers gaze,
And pausing buffaloes forget to graze;
Admiring elephants forsake their woods,
Stretch their wide ears, and wade into the floods;
In silent herds the wondering sea-calves lave,
Or nod their slimy foreheads o'er the wave;
Poised on still wing attentive vultures sweep,
And winking crocodiles are lull'd to sleep.]

" Where leads the northern star his lucid train
High o'er the snow-clad earth, and icy main,
With milky light the white horizon streams,
And to the Moon each sparkling mountain gleams.
Slow o'er the printed snows with silent walk
Huge shaggy forms across the twilight stalk;
And ever and anon with hideous sound
Burst the thick ribs of ice, and thunder round.
There, as old Winter flaps his hoary wing,
And lingering leaves his empire to the Spring,
Pierced with quick shafts of silver-shooting light
Fly, in dark troops, the dazzled imps of night.
'Awake, my Love!' enamour'd Muschus[100] cries,
'Stretch thy fair limbs, refulgent maid! arise,
Ope thy sweet eyelids to the rising ray,
And hail with ruby lips returning day.
Down the white hills dissolving torrents pour;
Green springs the turf, and purple blows the flower;
His torpid wing the Rail exulting tries,
Mounts the soft gale, and wantons in the skies;
Rise, let us mark how bloom the awaken'd groves,
'And 'mid the banks of roses *hide* our loves.'

" Night's tinsel beams on smooth Loch Lomond dance;
Impatient Aega[101] views the bright expanse.
In vain her eyes the passing floods explore:
Wave after wave rolls freightless to the shore.
Now dim amid the distant foam she spies
A rising speck: ''Tis he, 'tis he!' she cries.

---

[100] Musc(h)us corallinus, coral moss
[101] Conferva aegagropila (itinerant aquatic plant, globular in form [ed.)

As with firm arms he beats the streams aside
And cleaves with rising chest the tossing tide,
With bended knee she prints the humid sands,
Upturns her glistening eyes, and spreads her hands.

''Tis he, 'tis he! my lord, my life, my love!
Slumber, ye winds; ye billows, cease to move!
Beneath his arms your buoyant plumage spread,
Ye swans! ye halcyons hover round his head!'
With eager step the boiling surf she braves,
And meets her refluent lover in the waves;
Loose o'er the flood her azure mantle swims,
And the clear stream betrays her snowy limbs.
So on her sea-girt tower fair Hero stood
At parting day, and mark'd the dashing flood;
While high in air, the glimmering rocks above,
Shone the bright lamp, the pilot-star of love.
With robe outspread, the wavering flame behind,
She kneels, and guards it from the shifting wind;
Breathes to her goddess all her vows, and guides
Her bold Leander o'er the dusky tides;
Wrings his wet hair, his briny bosom warms,
And clasps her panting lover in her arms.

" Deep in wide caverns and their shadowy aisles,
Daughter of Earth, the chaste Truffelia[102] smiles;
On silvery beds, of soft asbestos wove,
Meets her Gnome-husband and avows her love.
High o'er her couch impending diamonds blaze,
And branching gold the crystal roof inlays;
With verdant light the modest emeralds glow,
Blue sapphires glare, and rubies blush, below;
Light piers of lazuli the dome surround,
And pictured mochoes tesselate the ground;
In glittering threads along reflective walls
The warm rill murmuring twinkles, as it falls;
Now sink the Eolian strings, and now they swell,
And Echoes woo in every vaulted cell;
While on white wings delighted Cupids play,
Shake their bright lamps, and shed celestial day.

" Closed in an azure fig by fairy spells,
Bosom'd in down, fair Capri-fica[103] dwells.

102 Lycoperdon tuber, truffle
103 Caprificus, wild fig

So sleeps in silence the Curculio[104], shut
In the dark chambers of the cavern'd nut,
Erodes with ivory beak the vaulted shell,
And quits on filmy wings its narrow cell.
(So the pleased linnet in the moss-wove nest
Waked into life beneath its parent's breast,
Chirps in the gaping shell, bursts forth erelong,
Shakes its new plumes, and tries its tender song.)
And now the talisman she strikes, that charms
Her husband-Sylph, and calls him to her arms.
Quick, the light gnat her airy lord bestrides,
With cobweb reins the flying courser guides,
From crystal steeps of viewless Ether springs,
Cleaves the soft air on still expanded wings;
Darts like a sunbeam o'er the boundless wave,
And seeks the beauty in her *secret* cave.
So with quick impulse through all nature's frame
Shoots the electric air its subtle flame;
So turns the impatient needle to the Pole,
Though mountains rise between, and oceans roll.

" Where round the Orcades white torrents roar,
Scooping with ceaseless rage the incumbent shore,
Wide o'er the deep a dusky cavern bends
Its marble arms, and high in air impends.
Basaltic piers the ponderous roof sustain,
And steep their massy sandals in the main;
Round the dim walls, and through the whispering aisles
Hoarse breathes the wind, the glittering water boils.
Here the charm'd Byssus with his blooming bride
Spreads his green sails, and braves the foaming tide;
The star of Venus gilds the twilight wave,
And lights her votaries to the *secret* cave;
Light Cupids flutter round the nuptial bed,
And each coy sea-maid hides her blushing head.

" Where cool'd by rills, and curtain'd round by woods,
Slopes the green dell to meet the briny floods,
(The sparkling noon-beams trembling on the tide)
The Proteus-lover[105] woos his playful bride:
To win the Fair he tries a thousand forms,
Basks on the sands, or gambols in the storms.

---

[104] Cynips psenes, a gnat
[105] Conferva polymorpha

A Dolphin now, his scaly sides he laves,
And bears the sportive damsel on the waves:
She strikes the cymbal as he moves along,
And wondering Ocean listens to the song.
And now a spotted Pard the lover stalks,
Plays round her steps, and guards her favour'd walks;
As with white teeth he prints her hand, caress'd,
And lays his velvet paw upon her breast,
O'er his round face her snowy fingers strain
The silken knots, and fit the ribbon-rein.
And now a Swan, he spreads his plumy sails,
And proudly glides before the fanning gales;
Pleased, on the flowery brink, with graceful hand
She waves her floating lover to the land.
Bright shines his sinuous neck; with crimson beak
He prints fond kisses on her glowing cheek;
Spreads his broad wings, elates his ebon crest,
And clasps the beauty to his downy breast.

" A *hundred* virgins join a *hundred* swains,
And fond Adonis[106] leads the sprightly trains;
Pair after pair, along his sacred groves
To Hymen's fane the bright procession moves.
Each smiling youth a myrtle garland shades,
And wreaths of roses veil the blushing maids;
Light Joys on twinkling feet attend the throng,
Weave the gay dance, or raise the frolic song.
Thick, as they pass, exulting Cupids fling
Promiscuous arrows from the sounding string.
On wings of gossamer soft Whispers fly,
And the sly Glance steals side-long from the eye.
As round his shrine the gaudy circles bow,
And seal with muttering lips the faithless vow,
Licentious Hymen joins their mingled hands,
And loosely twines the meretricious bands.
Thus where pleased Venus, in the southern main,
Sheds all her smiles on Otaheite's plain,
Wide o'er the isle her silken net she draws,
And the Loves laugh at all but Nature's laws."

Here ceased the Goddess. O'er the silent strings
Applauding zephyrs swept their fluttering wings;
Enraptured Sylphs arose in murmuring crowds
To air-wove canopies and pillowy clouds;

---

106 Adonis vernalis [ed.]

Each Gnome reluctant sought his earthy cell,
And each fair Floret closed her velvet bell.
Then, on soft tiptoe, Night approaching near
Hung o'er the tuneless lyre his sable ear,
Gemm'd with bright stars the still, ethereal plain,
And bade his Nightingales repeat the strain.

End of Canto Four

Part Three

THE TEMPLE OF NATURE
or
THE ORIGIN OF SOCIETY[1]

(An Evolutionary Scenario)

[Preamble to Canto One]

1 By firm immutable immortal laws
Impress'd on Nature by the Great First Cause,
Say, Muse![2] how rose from elemental strife
Organic forms, and kindled into life.
How Love and Sympathy with potent charm
Warm the cold heart, the lifted hand disarm,
Allure with pleasures, and alarm with pains,
And bind Society in golden chains.

Four past eventful Ages then recite,
And give the fifth, new-born of Time, to light;
The silken tissue of their joys disclose,
Swell with deep chords the murmur of their woes;
Their laws, their labours, and their loves proclaim,
And chant their virtues to the trump of Fame.

Immortal Love! who, ere the morn of Time,
On wings outstretch'd, o'er Chaos hung sublime;
Warm'd into life the bursting egg of Night,
And gave young Nature to admiring Light!
You! whose wide arms, in soft embraces furl'd
Round the vast frame, connect the whirling world!
Whether immersed in day, the Sun your throne,
You gird the planets in your silver zone;
Or warm, descending on ethereal wing,
The Earth's cold bosom with the beams of Spring;
Press drop to drop, to atom atom bind,
Link sex to sex, or rivet mind to mind;
Attend my song! With rosy lips rehearse,
And with your polish'd arrows write my verse!

---

[1] This is Darwin's original title which was changed to the less provocative 'The Temple of Nature' by the publisher, Joseph Johnson.
[2] The Muse here addressed by the poet is, perhaps, Clio, the muse of history and of epic poetry. She is the sister-muse to Urania, muse of astronomy and both preside over the natural sciences [ed.]

So shall my lines soft-rolling eyes engage,
And snow-white fingers turn the volant page;
The smiles of Beauty all my toils repay,
And youths and virgins chant the living lay.

2 Where Eden's sacred bowers triumphant sprung,
By angels guarded and by prophets sung,
Waved o'er the east in purple pride unfurl'd,
And rock'd the golden cradle of the world,
Four sparkling currents laved with wandering tides
Their velvet avenues and flowery sides;
On sun-bright lawns, unclad the Graces[3] stray'd,
And guiltless Cupids haunted every glade;
Till the fair Bride, forbidden shades among,
Heard unalarm'd the Tempter's serpent tongue,
Eyed the sweet fruit, the mandate disobey'd,
And her fond Lord with sweeter smiles betray'd.
Conscious awhile with throbbing heart he strove,
Spread his wide arms, and barter'd life for love.

Now rocks on rocks, in savage grandeur roll'd,
Steep above steep, the blasted plains infold;
The incumbent crags eternal tempest shrouds,
And livid lightnings cleave the lambent clouds;
Round the firm base loud-howling whirlwinds blow,
And sands in burning eddies dance below.

Hence ye profane! the warring winds exclude
Unhallow'd throngs that press with footstep rude;
But court the Muse's train with milder skies,
And call with softer voice the good and wise.

Charm'd at her touch the opening wall divides,
And rocks of crystal form the polish'd sides;
Through the bright arch the Loves and Graces tread,
Innocuous thunders murmuring o'er their head;
Pair after pair, and tittering as they pass,
View their fair features in the walls of glass;
Leave with impatient step the circling bourn,
And hear behind the closing rocks return.

Here, high in air, unconscious of the storm,
Thy Temple, Nature, rears its mystic form;

---

3 Attendants on Venus and the Muses [JD]. The Three Graces (Aglaia, Euphrosyne, and Thalia) represent fertility. [ed.]

From earth to heaven, unwrought by mortal toil,
Towers the vast fabric on the desert soil;
O'er many a league the ponderous domes extend,
And deep in earth the ribbed vaults descend;
A thousand jasper steps with circling sweep
Lead the slow votary up the winding steep;
Ten thousand piers, now join'd and now aloof,
Bear on their branching arms the fretted roof.

Unnumber'd aisles connect unnumber'd halls,
And sacred symbols crowd the pictured walls;
With pencil rude forgotten days design,
And arts, or empires, live in every line;
While, chain'd reluctant on the marble ground,
Indignant Time reclines, by Sculpture bound,
And sternly bending o'er a scroll unroll'd,
Inscribes the future with his style of gold.
So erst, when Proteus on the briny shore
New forms assumed of eagle, pard, or boar,
The wise Atrides bound in seaweed thongs
The changeful god amid his scaly throngs,
Till in deep tones his opening lips at last
Reluctant told the future and the past.

Here, o'er piazza'd courts and long arcades,
The bowers of Pleasure root their waving shades;
Shed o'er the pansied moss a chequer'd gloom,
Bend with new fruits, with flowers successive bloom.
Pleased, their light limbs on beds of roses press'd,
In slight undress recumbent Beauties rest;
On tiptoe steps surrounding Graces move,
And gay Desires expand their wings above.

Here young Dione arms her quiver'd Loves,
Schools her bright Nymphs, and practises her doves;
Calls round her laughing eyes in playful turns
The glance that lightens, and the smile that burns;
Her dimpling cheeks with transient blushes dyes,
Heaves her white bosom with seductive sighs,
Or moulds with rosy lips the magic words
That bind the heart in adamantine cords.

Behind, in twilight gloom, with scowling mien
The demon Pain convokes his court unseen.
Whips, fetters, flames, portray'd on sculptured stone,
In dread festoons adorn his ebon throne.

**Each side a cohort of Diseases stands,
And shuddering Fever leads the ghastly bands;
O'er all Despair expands his raven wings,
And guilt-stain'd Conscience darts a thousand stings.**

**Deep-whelm'd beneath, in vast sepulchral caves,
Oblivion dwells among unlabell'd graves;
The storied tomb, the laurell'd bust o'erturns,
And shakes their ashes from the mouldering urns.
No vernal Zephyr breathes, no sunbeams cheer,
Nor song nor simper ever enters here;
O'er the green floor and round the dew-damp wall,
The slimy snail and bloated lizard crawl;
While on white heaps of intermingled bones
The Muse of Melancholy sits and moans;
Showers her cold tears o'er Beauty's early wreck,
Spreads her pale arms and bends her marble neck.
So in rude rocks, beside the Aegean wave,
Trophonius scoop'd his sorrow-sacred cave;
Unbarr'd to pilgrim feet the brazen door,
And the sad sage returning smiled no more.**

**Shrined in the midst, majestic Nature stands,
Extends o'er earth and sea her hundred hands.
Tower upon tower her beamy forehead crests,
And births unnumber'd milk her hundred breasts;
Drawn round her brows a lucid veil depends;
O'er her fine waist the purfled[4] woof descends;
Her stately limbs the gather'd folds surround
And spread their golden selvage on the ground.**

**From this first altar famed Eleusis stole
Her secret symbols and her mystic scroll;
With pious fraud in after ages rear'd
Her gorgeous Temple, and the gods revered.
First, in dim pomp before the astonish'd throng,
Silence and Night and Chaos stalk'd along;
Dread scenes of Death, in nodding sables dress'd,
Froze the broad eye, and thrill'd the unbreathing breast.
Then the young Spring, with winged Zephyr, leads
The queen of Beauty to the blossom'd meads;
Charm'd, in her train admiring Hymen moves,
And tiptoe Graces hand in hand with Loves.**

---

[4] decorated along the edge [ed.]

Next while on pausing step the Masked Mimes
Enact the triumphs of forgotten times,
Conceal from vulgar throngs the mystic truth,
Or charm with Wisdom's lore the initiate youth;
Each shifting scene some patriot hero trod,
Some sainted beauty, or some saviour god.

3 Now rose in purple pomp the breezy dawn,
And crimson dew-drops trembled on the lawn;
Blazed high in air the Temple's golden vanes,
And dancing shadows veer'd upon the plains.
Long trains of virgins from the sacred grove,
Pair after pair in bright procession move;
With flower-fill'd baskets round the altar throng,
Or swing their censers as they wind along.
The fair Urania leads the blushing bands;
Presents their offerings with unsullied hands;
Pleased, to their dazzled eyes in part unshrouds
The Goddess-form; the rest is hid in clouds.

" Priestess of Nature![5] while with pious awe
Thy votary bends, the mystic veil withdraw;
Charm after charm, succession bright, display,
And give the Goddess to adoring day!
So kneeling realms shall own the power divine,
And Heaven and Earth pour incense on her shrine.

" Oh grant the Muse with pausing step to press
Each sun-bright avenue and green recess;
Led by thy hand survey the trophied walls,
The statued galleries and the pictured halls;
Scan the proud pyramid, and arch sublime,
Earth-canker'd urn, medallion green with time;
Stern busts of gods, with helmed heroes mix'd,
And Beauty's radiant forms that smile betwixt.
Waked by thy voice, transmuted by thy wand[6],
Their lips shall open and their arms expand;
The love-lost lady, and the warrior slain,
Leap from their tombs and sigh, or fight, again.

" So when ill-fated Orpheus tuned to woe
His potent lyre, and sought the realms below,

---

[5] i.e. Urania. The Muse is speaking. [ed.]
[6] Urania traditionally caried a pair of geometer's compasses. [ed.]

Charm'd into life unreal forms respired,
And listening Shades the dulcet notes admired.
Love led the sage through Death's tremendous porch,
Cheer'd with his smile and lighted with his torch.
Hell's triple dog his playful jaws expands,
Fawns round the god and licks his baby hands.
In wondering groups the shadowy nations throng,
And sigh, or simper, as he steps along:
Sad swains and nymphs forlorn on Lethe's brink
Hug their past sorrows, and refuse to drink.
Night's dazzled empress feels the golden flame
Play round her breast and melt her frozen frame;
Charms with soft words and soothes with amorous wiles
Her iron-hearted lord; and Pluto smiles.
His trembling bride the bard triumphant led
From the pale mansions of the astonish'd dead;
Gave the fair phantom to admiring Light:
Ah, soon again to tread irremeable night!"

[Canto One]

Production of Life

4 Her snow-white arm, indulgent to my song,
Waves the fair Hierophant[7], and moves along.
High plumes, that bending shade her amber hair,
Nod, as she steps, their silver leaves in air;
Bright chains of pearl, with golden buckles braced,
Clasp her white neck and zone her slender waist.
Thin folds of silk in soft meanders wind
Down her fine form, and undulate behind:
The purple border, on the pavement roll'd,
Swells in the gale and spreads its fringe of gold.

" First, if you can, celestial guide! disclose
From what fair fountain mortal life arose;
Whence the fine nerve to move and feel assign'd,
Contractile fibre, and ethereal mind.

" How Love and Sympathy the bosom warm,
Allure with pleasure, and with pain alarm;

[7] The 'fair Hierophant' (an interpreter of mysteries) is Urania. The Muse speaks in lines 215-22. [ed.]

With soft affections weave the social plan,
And charm the listening savage into Man."

"God the First Cause! In this terrene abode,
Young Nature lisps she is the child of God.
From embryon births her changeful forms improve,
Grow as they live, and strengthen as they move.

" Ere Time began, from flaming Chaos hurl'd,
Rose the bright spheres which form the circling world;
Earths from each sun with quick explosions burst,
And second planets issued from the first.
Then, whilst the sea at their coeval birth,
Surge over surge, involved the shoreless Earth,
Nursed by warm sun-beams in primeval caves,
Organic Life began beneath the waves.

" First Heat from chemic dissolution springs,
And gives to Matter its eccentric wings;
With strong Repulsion parts the exploding mass,
Melts into lymph[8], or kindles into gas.
Attraction next (as earth or air subsides)
The ponderous atoms from the light divides;
Approaching parts[9] with quick embrace combines,
Swells into spheres, and lengthens into lines.
Last, as fine goads the gluten-threads excite,
Cords grapple cords, and webs with webs unite;
And quick Contraction with ethereal flame
Lights into life the fibre-woven frame.
Hence without parent, by spontaneous birth,
Rise the first specks of animated earth;
From Nature's womb the plant or insect swims,
And buds or breathes, with microscopic limbs.

" In earth, sea, air, around, below, above,
Life's subtle woof in Nature's loom is wove;
Points glued to points a living line extends,
Touch'd by some goad approach the bending ends.
Rings join to rings, and irritated tubes
Clasp with young lips the nutrient globes or cubes,
And, urged by appetencies new, select,
Imbibe, retain, digest, secrete, eject.

---

8 a pure transparent fluid [JD]
9 i.e. particles [ed.]

In branching cones, the living web expands:
Lymphatic ducts, and convoluted glands.
Aortal tubes propel the nascent blood,
And lengthening veins absorb the refluent flood.
Leaves, lungs, and gills the vital ether breathe,
On Earth's green surface, or the waves beneath.
So Life's first powers arrest the winds and floods:
To bones convert them, or to shells, or woods;
Stretch the vast beds of argil[10], lime, and sand,
And from diminish'd oceans form the land.

" Next the long nerves unite their silver train,
And young Sensation permeates the brain;
Through each new sense the keen emotions dart,
Flush the young cheek, and swell the throbbing heart.
From pain and pleasure quick Volitions rise:
Lift the strong arm, or point the inquiring eyes;
With Reason's light bewilder'd Man direct,
And right and wrong with balance nice detect.
Last, in thick swarms Associations spring:
Thoughts join to thoughts, to motions motions cling;
Whence in long trains of catenation[11] flow
Imagined joy and voluntary woe.

" So, view'd through crystal spheres, in drops saline
Quick-shooting salts in chemic forms combine;
Or Mucor stems, a vegetative tribe,
Spread their fine roots, the tremulous wave imbibe.
Next to our wondering eyes the focus brings
Self-moving lines and animated rings.
First Monas moves: an unconnected point
Plays round the drop without a limb or joint;
Then Vibrio waves with capillary eels[12],
And Vorticella whirls her living wheels,
While insect Proteus sports with changeful form
Through the bright tide: a globe, a cube, a worm.
Last o'er the field the Mite enormous swims,
Swells his red heart, and writhes his giant limbs.

5 " Organic Life beneath the shoreless waves
Was born and nursed in Ocean's pearly caves.

---

[10] potter's clay [JD]
[11] regular connection, link [JD]
[12] i.e. undulating hairs [ed.]

First, forms minute, unseen by spheric glass,
Move on the mud, or pierce the watery mass.
These, as successive generations bloom,
New powers acquire, and larger limbs assume;
Whence countless groups of vegetation spring,
And breathing realms of fin, and feet, and wing.

" Thus, the tall oak, the giant of the wood,
Which bears Britannia's thunders on the flood;
The whale, unmeasured monster of the main;
The lordly lion, monarch of the plain;
The eagle soaring in the realms of air,
Whose eye undazzled drinks the solar glare;
Imperious man, who rules the bestial crowd,
Of language, reason, and reflection proud,
With brow erect who scorns this earthy sod,
And styles himself the image of his God;
Arose from rudiments of form and sense,
An embryon point, or microscopic ens!

" Now in vast shoals beneath the brineless tide,
On Earth's firm crust testaceous tribes reside;
Age after age expands the peopled plain:
The tenants perish, but their cells remain;
Whence coral walls and sparry hills ascend
From Pole to Pole, and round the Line extend.

" Next, when imprison'd fires in central caves
Burst the firm earth, and drink the headlong waves;
And, as new airs with dread explosion swell,
Form lava-isles, and continents of shell;
Pile rocks on rocks, on mountains mountains raise,
And high in heaven the first volcanoes blaze;
In countless swarms an insect-myriad moves
From sea-fan gardens and from coral groves,
Leaves the cold caverns of the deep, and creeps
On shelving shores, or climbs on rocky steeps.
As in dry air the sea-born stranger roves,
Each muscle quickens, and each sense improves:
Cold gills aquatic form respiring lungs,
And sounds aerial flow from slimy tongues.

" So Trapa, rooted in pellucid tides,
In countless threads her breathing leaves divides,
Waves her bright tresses in the watery mass,
And drinks with gelid gills the vital gas;

Then broader leaves in shadowy files advance,
Spread o'er the crystal flood their green expanse,
And, as in air the adherent dew exhales,
Court the warm sun, and breathe ethereal gales.

"So still the tadpole cleaves the watery vale
With balanced fins and undulating tail;
New lungs and limbs proclaim his second birth,
Breathe the dry air, and bound upon the earth.

"So from deep lakes the dread mosquito springs,
Drinks the soft breeze, and dries his tender wings;
In twinkling squadrons cuts his airy way,
Dips his red trunk in blood, and Man his prey.

"So still the diodons (amphibious tribe)
With two-fold lungs the sea or air imbibe;
Allied to fish, the lizard cleaves the flood
With one-cell'd heart and dark frigescent[13] blood;
Half-reasoning beavers long-unbreathing dart
Through Erie's waves with perforated heart;
With gills and lungs respiring lampreys steer,
Kiss the rude rocks, and suck till they adhere;
The lazy remora's inhaling lips
Hung on the keel retard the struggling ships;
With gills pulmonic breathes the enormous whale,
And spouts aquatic columns to the gale,
Sports on the shining wave at noontide hours,
And shifting rainbows crest the rising showers.

"So erst, ere rose the science to record
In letter'd syllables the volant word,
Whence chemic arts, disclosed in pictured lines,
Lived to mankind by hieroglyphic signs,
And clustering stars, portray'd on mimic spheres,
Assumed the forms of lions, bulls, and bears.
So erst, as Egypt's rude designs explain,
Rose young Dione from the shoreless main.
Type of organic Nature! source of bliss!
Emerging Beauty from the vast abyss!
Sublime, on Chaos borne, the goddess stood,
And smiled enchantment on the troubled flood;
The warring elements to peace restored,
And young Reflection wondered and adored."

---

13 cooling [ed.]

Now paus'd the Nymph. The Muse, responsive, cries
(Sweet admiration sparkling in her eyes):
" Drawn by your pencil, by your hand unfurl'd,
Bright shines the tablet of the dawning world.
Amazed, the sea's prolific depths I view,
And Venus rising from the waves, in you!

" Still, Nature's births, enclosed in egg or seed,
From the tall forest to the lowly weed,
Her beaux and beauties, butterflies and worms,
Rise from aquatic to aerial forms.
Thus in the womb the nascent infant laves
Its natant form in the circumfluent waves;
With perforated heart unbreathing swims,
Awakes and stretches all its recent limbs;
With gills placental seeks the arterial flood,
And drinks pure ether from its mother's blood.
Erewhile, the landed Stranger bursts his way,
From the warm wave emerging into day;
Feels the chill blast, and piercing light, and tries
His tender lungs, and rolls his dazzled eyes;
Gives to the passing gale his curling hair,
And steps a dry inhabitant of air.

" Creative Nile, as taught in ancient song,
So charm'd to life his animated throng.
O'er his wide realms the slow-subsiding flood
Left the rich treasures of organic mud;
While with quick growth young Vegetation yields
Her blushing orchards and her waving fields:
Pomona's hand replenish'd Plenty's horn,
And Ceres laugh'd amid her seas of corn.
Bird, beast and reptile spring from sudden birth,
Raise their new forms: half-animal, half-earth.
The roaring lion shakes his tawny mane,
His struggling limbs still rooted in the plain;
With flapping wings assurgent eagles toil
To rend their talons from the adhesive soil;
The impatient serpent lifts his crested head,
And drags his train unfinish'd from the bed.
As Warmth and Moisture blend their magic spells,
And brood with mingling wings the slimy dells,
Contractile earths in sentient forms arrange,
And Life triumphant stays their chemic change."

Then hand in hand along the waving glades
The virgin Sisters pass beneath the shades,

Ascend the winding steps with pausing march,
And seek the portico's susurrant arch:
Whose sculptured architrave, on columns borne,
Drinks the first blushes of the rising morn;
Whose fretted roof an ample shield displays,
And guards the Beauties from meridian rays;
While on light step enamour'd Zephyr springs,
And fans their glowing features with his wings,
Imbibes the fragrance of the vernal flowers,
And speeds with kisses sweet the dancing Hours.

Urania, leaning with unstudied grace,
Rests her white elbow on a column's base;
Awhile reflecting, takes her silent stand,
Her fair cheek press'd upon her lily hand.
Then, as awaking from ideal trance[14],
On the smooth floor her pausing steps advance;
Waves high her arm, upturns her lucid eyes,
Marks the wide scenes of ocean, earth, and skies,
And leads, meandering as it rolls along
Through Nature's walks, the shining stream of song.

First her sweet voice in plaintive accents chains
The Muse's ear with fascinating strains;
Reverts awhile to elemental strife,
The change of form, and brevity of life;
Then tells how potent Love with torch sublime
Re-lights the glimmering lamp, and conquers Time.
The polish'd walls reflect her rosy smiles,
And sweet-toned echoes talk along the aisles.

End of Canto One

[14] a kind of reverie [ed.]; the state of mind in which 'by the art of the painter or poet a train of ideas is suggested to our imagination' [ED], "The Loves of the Plants", Interlude One.

Canto Two

Reproduction of Life

" How short the span of Life! some hours possess'd,
Warm but to cool, and active but to rest!
The age-worn fibres goaded to contract,
By repetition palsied, cease to act!
When Time's cold hands the languid senses seize,
Chill the dull nerves, the lingering currents freeze,
Organic matter, unreclaim'd by Life,
Reverts to elements by chemic strife.
Thus heat evolved from some fermenting mass
Expands the kindling atoms into gas,
Which sinks ere long in cold concentric rings,
Condensed on Gravity's descending wings.

" But Reproduction, with ethereal fires,
New life rekindles ere the first expires:
Calls up renascent Youth ere tottering Age
Quits the dull scene, and gives him to the stage;
Bids on his cheek the rose of beauty blow,
And binds the wreaths of pleasure round his brow;
With finer links the vital chain extends,
And the long line of Being never ends.

" Self-moving Engines by unbending springs
May walk on earth, or flap their mimic wings;
In tubes of glass mercurial columns rise
Or sink, obedient to the incumbent skies[15];
Or, as they touch the figured scale, repeat
The nice gradations of circumfluent heat.
But Reproduction, when the perfect elf
Forms from fine glands another like itself,
Gives the true character of life and sense,
And parts the organic from the chemic ens.
Where milder skies protect the nascent brood,
And Earth's warm bosom yields salubrious food,
Each new descendant with superior powers
Of sense and motion speeds the transient hours;
Braves every season, tenants every clime,
And Nature rises on the wings of Time.

---

[15] i.e. atmospheric pressure [ed.]

" As Life discordant elements arrests,
Rejects the noxious and the pure digests,
Combines with heat the fluctuating mass,
And gives awhile solidity to gas,
Organic forms with chemic changes strive,
Live but to die, and die but to revive.
Immortal matter braves the transient storm,
Mounts from the wreck unchanging but in form.

" So, as the Sages of the East record
In sacred symbol or unletter'd word,
Emblem of Life, to change eternal doom'd,
The beauteous form of fair Adonis bloom'd.
On Syrian hills the graceful hunter slain
Dyed with his gushing blood the shuddering plain,
And slow-descending to the Elysian shade
Awhile with Proserpine reluctant stray'd.
Soon from the yawning grave the bursting clay
Restored the Beauty to delighted day,
Array'd in youth's resuscitated charms;
And young Dione woo'd him to her arms.
Pleased for a while, the assurgent youth above
Relights the golden lamp of Life and Love.
Ah! soon again to leave the cheerful light,
And sink alternate to the realms of Night.

2 " Hence, ere vitality, as time revolves,
Leaves the cold organ, and the mass dissolves,
The reproductions of the living ens
From sires to sons, unknown to sex, commence.
New buds and bulbs the living fibre shoots
On lengthening branches and protruding roots;
Or on the father's side from bursting glands
The adhering young its nascent form expands;
In branching lines the parent-trunk adorns,
And parts ere long like plumage, hairs, or horns.

" So the lone truffle, lodged beneath the earth,
Shoots from paternal roots the tuberous birth;
No stamen-males ascend and breathe above,
No seed-born offspring lives by female love.
From each young tree, for future buds design'd,
Organic drops exude beneath the rind;

While these with appetencies[16] nice invite,
And those with apt propensities unite;
New embryon fibrils round the trunk combine
With quick embrace, and form the living line;
Whose plume and rootlet at their early birth
Seek the dry air, or pierce the humid earth.

" So safe in waves prolific volvox dwells,
And five descendants crowd his lucid cells;
So the male polypus parental swims,
And branching infants bristle all his limbs;
So the lone taenia[17] as he grows, prolongs
His flatten'd form with young adherent throngs;
Unknown to sex, the pregnant oyster swells,
And coral-insects build their radiate shells.
Parturient sires caress their infant train,
And heaven-born Storge[18] weaves the social chain:
Successive births her tender cares combine,
And soft affections live along the line.

" On angel-wings the Goddess Form descends,
Round her fond broods her silver arms she bends;
White streams of milk her tumid bosom swell,
And on her lips ambrosial kisses dwell.
Light Joys on twinkling feet before her dance
With playful nod and momentary glance;
Behind, attendant on the pansied plain,
Young Psyche treads, with Cupid in her train.

3 " In these lone births, no tender mothers blend
Their genial powers to nourish or defend;
No nutrient streams from Beauty's orbs improve
These orphan babes of solitary love.
Birth after birth the line unchanging runs,
And fathers live transmitted in their sons.
Each passing year beholds the unvarying kinds,
The same their manners and the same their minds,
Till, as erelong successive buds decay
And insect-shoals successive pass away,
Increasing wants the pregnant parents vex
With the fond wish to form a softer sex,

---

[16] strong or sensual desires [JD]
[17] the tape-worm
[18] instinctive parental love [ed.]

Whose milky rills with pure ambrosial food
Might charm and cherish their expected brood.
The potent wish in the productive hour
Calls to its aid Imagination's power:
O'er embryon throngs with mystic charm presides,
And sex from sex the nascent world divides;
With soft affections warms the callow trains,
And gives to laughing Love his nymphs and swains,
Whose mingling virtues interweave at length
The mother's beauty with the father's strength.

" So tulip-bulbs emerging from the seed,
Year after year unknown to sex proceed;
Erewhile the stamens and the styles display
Their petal-curtains, and adorn the day;
The beaux and beauties in each blossom glow
With wedded joy, or amatorial woe.
Unmarried aphides prolific prove
For nine successions uninform'd of love;
New sexes next with softer passions spring,
Breathe the fond vow, and woo with quivering wing.

" So erst in Paradise creation's Lord,
As the first leaves of holy writ record,
From Adam's rib (who press'd the flowery grove
And dreamt delighted of untasted love
To cheer and charm his solitary mind)
Form'd a new sex, the Mother of Mankind.
Buoy'd on light step the Beauty seem'd to swim,
And stretch'd alternate every pliant limb;
Pleased on Euphrates's velvet margin stood,
And view'd her playful image in the flood;
Own'd the fine flame of love, as life began,
And smiled enchantment on adoring Man.
Down her white neck, and o'er her bosom roll'd,
Flow'd in sweet negligence her locks of gold;
Round her fine form the dim transparence play'd,
And show'd the beauties that it seem'd to shade.
Enamour'd Adam gazed with fond surprise,
And drank delicious passion from her eyes;
Felt the new thrill of young Desire, and press'd
The graceful Virgin to his glowing breast.
The conscious Fair betrays her soft alarms,
Sinks with warm blush into his closing arms,
Yields to his fond caress with wanton play
And sweet, reluctant, amorous delay.

" Where no new sex with glands nutritious feeds,
Nursed in her womb the solitary breeds[19];
No Mother's care their early steps directs,
Warms in her bosom, with her wings protects.
The clime unkind, or noxious food, instils
To embryon nerves hereditary ills;
The feeble births acquired diseases chase,
Till Death extinguish the degenerate race.

" So grafted trees with shadowy summits rise,
Spread their fair blossoms and perfume the skies;
Till canker taints the vegetable blood,
Mines round the bark, and feeds upon the wood.
So years successive, from perennial roots
The wire or bulb with lessen'd vigour shoots;
Till curled leaves, or barren flowers, betray
A waning lineage verging to decay;
Or till, amended by connubial powers,
Rise seedling progenies from sexual flowers.

" E'en where unmix'd the breed, in sexual tribes
Parental taints the nascent babe imbibes:
Eternal war the Gout and Mania wage
With fierce, uncheck'd, hereditary rage;
Sad Beauty's form foul Scrofula surrounds
With bones distorted and putrescent wounds;
And, fell Consumption! thy unerring dart
Wets its broad wing in Youth's reluctant heart.

" With pausing step, at night's refulgent noon,
Beneath the sparkling stars and lucid moon,
Plunged in the shade of some religious tower
(The slow bell counting the departed hour)
O'er gaping tombs where shed umbrageous yews
On mouldering bones their cold unwholesome dews,
While low aerial voices whisper round,
And moon-drawn spectres dance upon the ground,
Poetic Melancholy loves to tread,
And bend in silence o'er the countless dead;
Marks, with loud sobs, infantine Sorrows rave,
And wring their pale hands o'er their mother's grave;

---

[19] These lines describe solitary reproduction in which the species has not yet evolved ('no new sex') the separate and specific organs (e.g. 'glands nutritious') of sexual reproduction. The solitary parent can be viewed as either maternal or paternal. [ed.]

Hears on the new-turn'd sod with gestures wild
The kneeling Beauty call her buried child,
Upbraid with timorous accents Heaven's decrees,
And with sad sighs augment the passing breeze.
'Stern Time,' she cries, 'receives from Nature's womb
Her beauteous births, and bears them to the tomb;
Calls all her sons from Earth's remotest bourn,
And from the closing portals none return!'"

5 Urania paused, upturn'd her streaming eyes,
And her white bosom heaved with silent sighs.
With her, the Muse laments the sum of things,
And hides her sorrows with her meeting wings.
Long o'er the wrecks of lovely Life they weep,
Then, pleased, reflect, 'to die is but to sleep'.
From Nature's coffins to her cradles turn,
Smile with young joy, with new affection burn.

And now the Muse, with mortal woes impress'd,
Thus the fair Hierophant again address'd:
'Ah me! celestial guide, thy words impart
Ills undeserved that rend the nascent heart!
O, Goddess, say, if brighter scenes improve
Air-breathing tribes, and births of sexual love?'
The smiling Fair obeys the inquiring Muse,
And in sweet tones her grateful task pursues.

" Now on broad pinions from the realms above
Descending Cupid seeks the Cyprian grove;
To his wide arms enamour'd Psyche springs,
And clasps her lover with aurelian wings.
A purple sash across his shoulder bends,
And fringed with gold the quiver'd shafts suspends;
The bending bow obeys the silken string,
And, as he steps, the silver arrows ring.
Thin folds of gauze with dim transparence flow
O'er her fair forehead and her neck of snow;
The winding woof her graceful limbs surrounds,
Swells in the breeze and sweeps the velvet grounds.
As hand in hand along the flowery meads
His blushing bride the quiver'd hero leads,
Charm'd round their heads pursuing Zephyrs throng,
And scatter roses as they move along;
Bright beams of Spring in soft effusion play,
And halcyon Hours invite them on their way.

“ Delighted Hymen hears their whisper’d vows,
And binds his chaplets round their polish’d brows;
Guides to his altar, ties the flowery bands,
And as they kneel, unites their willing hands.
‘Behold!,’ he cries, ‘Earth! Ocean! Air above!
And hail the Deities of Sexual Love!
All forms of life shall this fond pair delight,
And sex to sex the willing world unite;
Shed their sweet smiles in Earth’s unsocial bowers,
Fan with soft gales, and gild with brighter hours;
Fill Pleasure’s chalice unalloy’d with pain,
And give Society his golden chain.’

“ Now young Desires, on purple pinions borne,
Mount the warm gales of manhood’s rising morn;
With softer fires through virgin bosoms dart,
Flush the pale cheek and goad the tender heart.
Ere the weak powers of transient life decay,
And Heaven’s ethereal image melts away,
Love, with nice touch, renews the organic frame,
Forms a young ens, another and the same;
Gives from his rosy lips the vital breath,
And parries with his hands the shafts of Death.
While Beauty broods, with angel-wings unfurl’d,
O’er nascent life, and saves the sinking world.

“ Hence on green leaves the sexual Pleasures dwell,
And Loves and Beauties crowd the blossom’s bell:
The wakeful Anther in his silken bed
O’er the pleased Stigma bows his waxen head;
With meeting lips and mingling smiles they sup
Ambrosial dewdrops from the nectar’d cup;
Or buoy’d in air the plumy Lover springs,
And seeks his panting Bride on Hymen-wings.

“ The Stamen-males, with appetencies just,
Produce a formative prolific dust;
With apt propensities, the Styles recluse
Secrete a formative prolific juice.
These in the Pericarp erewhile arrive,
Rush to each other, and embrace alive.
Form’d by new powers, progressive parts succeed,
Join in one whole, and swell into a seed.

“ So in fond swarms the living Anthers shine
Of bright Vallisner on the wavy Rhine;

Break from their stems, and on the liquid glass
Surround the admiring Stigmas as they pass.
The love-sick Beauties lift their essenced brows,
Sigh to the Cyprian Queen their secret vows,
Like watchful Hero feel their soft alarms,
And clasp their floating Lovers in their arms.

" Hence the male ants their gauzy wings unfold,
And young Lampyris[20] waves his plumes of gold;
The glow-worm sparkles with impassion'd light
On each green bank, and charms the eye of Night;
While new desires the painted snail perplex,
And twofold love unites the double sex.

" Hence, when the Morus[21] in Italia's lands
To Spring's warm beam its timid leaf expands,
The silk-worm broods, in countless tribes above,
Crop the green treasure, uninform'd of love.
Erewhile, the changeful worm with circling head
Weaves the nice curtains of his silken bed:
Web within web involves his larva-form,
Alike secured from sunshine and from storm.
For twelve long days he dreams of blossom'd groves,
Untasted honey, and ideal Loves;
Wakes from his trance alarm'd with young Desire,
Finds his new sex, and feels ecstatic fire.
From flower to flower with honey'd lip he springs,
And seeks his velvet Loves on silver wings.

6 " The demon Jealousy, with Gorgon frown,
Blasts the sweet flowers of Pleasure not his own;
Rolls his wild eyes, and through the shuddering grove
Pursues the steps of unsuspecting Love;
Or drives o'er rattling plains his iron car,
Flings his red torch, and lights the flames of war.

" Here cocks heroic burn with rival rage,
And quails with quails in doubtful fight engage:
Of armed heels and bristling plumage proud,
They sound the insulting clarion shrill and loud;
With rustling pinions meet, and swelling chests,
And seize with closing beaks their bleeding crests;

---

20 firefly
21 mulberry [ed.]

Rise on quick wing above the struggling foe,
And aim in air the death-devoting blow.
There the hoarse stag his croaking rival scorns,
And butts and parries with his branching horns.
Contending boars with tusk enamell'd strike,
And guard with shoulder-shield the blow oblique,
While female bands attend in mute surprise,
And view the victor with admiring eyes.

" So knight on knight, recorded in romance,
Urged the proud steed and couch'd the extended lance.
He, whose dread prowess with resistless force
O'erthrew the opposing warrior and his horse,
Bless'd[22], as the golden guerdon[23] of his toils,
Bowed to the Beauty, and received her smiles.

" So when fair Helen with ill-fated charms,
By Paris wooed, provoked the world to arms;
Left her vindictive Lord to sigh in vain
For broken vows, lost love, and cold disdain.
Fired at his wrongs, associate to destroy
The realms unjust of proud adulterous Troy,
Unnumber'd heroes braved the dubious fight,
And sunk lamented to the shades of night.

" Now vows connubial chain the plighted pair,
And join paternal with maternal care:
The married birds with nice selection cull
Soft thistle-down, grey moss, and scattered wool;
Line the secluded nest with feathery rings,
Meet with fond bills, and woo with fluttering wings.
Week after week, regardless of her food,
The incumbent Linnet warms her future brood:
Each spotted egg with ivory lips she turns,
Day after day with fond expectance burns,
Hears the young prisoner chirping in his cell,
And breaks in hemispheres the obdurate shell.
Loud trills sweet Philomel his tender strain,
Charms his fond bride, and wakes his infant train;
Perch'd on the circling moss, the listening throng
Wave their young wings and whisper to the song.

---

[22] i.e. favoured [ed.]
[23] reward, recompense [JD]

" The lion-king forgets his savage pride
And courts with playful paws his tawny bride;
The listening tiger hears with kindling flame
The love-lorn night-call of his brinded dame.
Despotic Love dissolves the bestial war,
Bends their proud necks, and joins them to his car;
Shakes o'er the obedient pairs his silken thong,
And goads the humble, or restrains the strong.
Slow roll the silver wheels (in beauty's pride
Celestial Psyche blushing by his side).
The lordly bull behind, and warrior horse,
With voice of thunder shake the echoing course;
Chain'd to the car with herds domestic move,
And swell the triumph of despotic Love.

" Pleased, as they pass along the breezy shore,
In twinkling shoals the scaly realms adore;
Move on quick fin with undulating train,
Or lift their slimy foreheads from the main.
High o'er their heads, on pinions broad display'd,
The feather'd nations shed a floating shade:
Pair after pair enamour'd shoot along,
And trill in air the gay impassion'd song.
With busy hum, in playful swarms around,
Emerging insects leave the peopled ground,
Rise in dark clouds and, borne in airy rings,
Sport round the car and wave their golden wings.
Admiring Fawns pursue on dancing hoof,
And bashful Dryads peep from shades aloof;
Emerging Nereids rise from coral cells;
Enamour'd Tritons sound their twisted shells;
From sparkling founts enchanted Naiads move,
And swell the triumph of despotic Love.

" Delighted Flora, gazing from afar,
Greets with mute homage the triumphal car;
On silvery slippers steps, with bosom bare,
Bends her white knee and bows her auburn hair;
Calls to her purple heaths and blushing bowers,
Bursts her green gems and opens all her flowers;
O'er the bright pair a shower of roses sheds,
And crowns with wreaths of hyacinth their heads.
Slow roll the silver wheels, with snowdrops deck'd,
And primrose-bands the cedar spokes connect;
Round the fine pole the twisting woodbine clings,
And knots of jasmine clasp the bending springs;
Bright daisy-links the velvet harness chain,

And rings of violets join each silken rein;
Festoon'd behind, the snow-white lilies bend,
And tulip-tassels on each side depend.
Slow rolls the car; the enamour'd flowers exhale
Their treasured sweets, and whisper to the gale;
Their ravell'd buds and wrinkled cups unfold;
Nod their green stems, and wave their bells of gold;
Breathe their soft sighs from each enchanted grove,
And hail the Deities of Sexual Love.

" Onward, with march sublime, in saffron robe
Young Hymen steps, and traverses the globe:
O'er burning sands and snow-clad mountains treads
Blue fields of air, and ocean's briny beds;
Flings from his radiant torch celestial light
O'er Day's wide concave, and illumes the Night.
With dulcet eloquence his tuneful tongue
Convokes and captivates the fair and young:
His golden lamp with ray ethereal dyes
The blushing cheek, and lights the laughing eyes;
With secret flames the virgin's bosom warms,
And lights the impatient bridegroom to her arms;
With lovely life all Nature's frame inspires,
And, as they sink, rekindles all her fires."

7 Now paused the beauteous Teacher, and awhile
Gazed on her train with sympathetic smile.
" Beware of Love!" she cried, "ye Nymphs, and hear
His twanging bowstring with alarmed ear;
Fly the first whisper of the distant dart,
Or shield with adamant the fluttering heart.
To secret shades, ye virgin trains, retire,
And in your bosoms guard the vestal fire."
The obedient Beauties hear her words, advised,
And bow with laugh repress'd and smile chastised.

Now at her nod the Nymphs attendant bring
Translucent water from the bubbling spring:
In crystal cups the waves salubrious shine,
Unstain'd, untainted with immodest wine.
Next where, emerging from its ancient roots,
Its widening boughs the Tree of Knowledge shoots,
Pluck'd with nice choice, before the Muse they placed
The now no longer interdicted taste.
Awhile they sit, from higher cares released,
And, pleased, partake the intellectual feast.

Of good and ill they speak, effect and cause,
Celestial agencies and Nature's laws.

So when angelic Forms to Syria sent
Sat in the cedar shade by Abraham's tent,
A spacious bowl the admiring Patriarch fills
With dulcet water from the scanty rills;
Sweet fruits and kernels gathers from his hoard;
With milk and butter piles the plenteous board;
While on the heated earth his Consort bakes
Fine flour well kneaded in unleaven'd cakes.
The guests ethereal quaff the lucid flood,
Smile on their hosts, and taste terrestrial food;
And, while from seraph-lips sweet converse springs,
Lave their fair feet and close their silver wings.

End of Canto Two

[Preamble to Canto Three]

Now rose, adorn'd with Beauty's brightest hues,
The graceful Hierophant and winged Muse.
Onward they step around the stately piles,
O'er porcelain floors, through laqueated[24] aisles;
Eye Nature's lofty and her lowly seats,
Her gorgeous palaces and green retreats;
Pervade her labyrinths with unerring tread,
And leave for future guests a guiding thread.

First, with fond gaze blue fields of air they sweep,
Or pierce the briny chambers of the deep;
Earth's burning Line and icy Poles explore,
Her fertile surface and her caves of ore;
Or mark how Oxygen with Azote-gas
Plays round the globe in one aerial mass,
Or, fused with Hydrogen, in ceaseless flow
Forms the wide waves which foam and roll below.

Next, with illumined hands through prisms bright,
Pleased they untwist the sevenfold threads of light;
Or, bent in pencils by the lens, convey
To one bright point the silver hairs of day.
Then mark how two electric streams conspire
To form the resinous and vitreous[25] fire;
Beneath the waves the fierce Gymnotus arm,
And give Torpedo his benumbing charm;
Or, through Galvanic chain-work[26] as they pass,
Convert the kindling water into gas.

How at the poles[27] opposing Ethers dwell,
Attract the quivering needle, or repel.
How gravitation, by immortal laws,
Surrounding matter to a centre draws.
How heat, pervading oceans, airs, and lands,
With force uncheck'd the mighty mass expands.
And last how, born in elemental strife
Beam'd the first spark, and lighten'd into Life.

---

[24] with panelled, or coffered, ceilings [ed.]
[25] negative and positive electricity
[26] i.e. Galvanic (later known as Voltaic [ed.]) Pile
[27] i.e. two magnetic poles [ed.]

Now in sweet tones the inquiring Muse express'd
Her ardent wish, and thus the Fair address'd:
" Priestess of Nature! whose exploring sight
Pierces the realms of Chaos and of Night;
Of space unmeasured marks the first and last,
Of endless time the present, future, past;
Immortal Guide! O, now with accents kind
Give to my ear the Progress of the Mind.
How loves, and tastes, and sympathies commence
From evanescent notices of sense?
How from the yielding touch and rolling eyes
The piles immense of human science rise?
With mind gigantic steps the puny elf,
And weighs and measures all things but himself!"

The indulgent Beauty hears the grateful Muse,
Smiles on her pupil, and her task renews.
Attentive Nymphs in sparkling squadrons throng,
And choral Virgins listen to the song;
Pleased Fawns and Naiads crowd in silent rings,
And hovering Cupids stretch their purple wings.

[Canto Three]

Progress of the Mind

2 " First the new actions of the excited sense,
Urged by appulses from without, commence;
With these exertions pain, or pleasure, springs,
And forms perceptions of external things.
Thus, when illumined by the solar beams,
Yon waving woods, green lawns, and sparkling streams,
In one bright point by rays converging lie
Planed on the moving tablet of the eye;
The mind obeys the silver goads of light,
And Irritation moves the nerves of sight.

" These acts repeated rise from joys or pains,
And swell Imagination's flowing trains;
So in dread dreams amid the silent night,
Grim spectre-forms the shuddering sense affright;
Or Beauty's idol-image, as it moves,
Charms the closed eye with graces, smiles, and loves;
Each passing form the pausing heart delights,
And young Sensation every nerve excites.

" Oft from Sensation quick Volition springs,
When pleasure thrills us, or when anguish stings.
Hence Recollection calls with voice sublime
Immersed ideas from the wrecks of Time;
With potent charm in lucid trains displays
Eventful stories of forgotten days.
Hence Reason's efforts good with ill contrast,
Compare the present, future, and the past,
Each passing moment, unobserved, restrain
The wild discordancies of Fancy's train,
But leave uncheck'd the night's ideal streams[28],
Or, sacred Muses! your meridian dreams.

" And last, Suggestion's mystic power describes
Ideal hosts arranged in trains or tribes.
So, when the Nymph with volant finger rings
Her dulcet harp and shakes the sounding strings;
As with soft voice she trills the enamour'd song,
Successive notes, unwill'd, the strain prolong;
The transient trains Association steers,
And sweet vibrations charm the astonish'd ears.

" On rapid feet o'er hills, and plains, and rocks,
Speed the scared leveret and rapacious fox;
On rapid pinions cleave the fields above
The hawk descending, and escaping dove;
With nicer nostril track the tainted ground
The hungry vulture, and the prowling hound;
Converge reflected light with nicer eye
The midnight owl, and microscopic fly;
With finer ear pursue their nightly course
The listening lion, and the alarmed horse.

" The branching forehead with diverging horns
Crests the bold bull, the jealous stag adorns;
Fierce rival boars with side-long fury wield
The pointed tusk, and guard with shoulder-shield;
Bounds the dread tiger o'er the affrighted heath,
Arm'd with sharp talons and resistless teeth;
The pouncing eagle bears in clinched claws
The struggling lamb, and rends with ivory jaws;
The tropic eel, electric in his ire,
Alarms the waves with unextinguish'd fire;

---

[28] i.e. flow of images and ideas in dreams [ed.]

The fly of night illumes his airy way
And seeks with lucid lamp his sleeping prey;
Fierce on his foe the poisoning serpent springs,
And insect armies dart their venom'd stings.

" Proud Man alone, in wailing weakness born,
No horns protect him, and no plumes adorn;
No finer powers of nostril, ear, or eye,
Teach the young reasoner to pursue or fly.
Nerved with fine touch above the bestial throngs,
The hand, first gift of Heaven! to Man belongs.
Untipt with claws the circling fingers close;
With rival points the bending thumbs oppose;
Trace the nice lines of Form with sense refined,
And clear ideas charm the thinking mind;
Whence the fine organs of the touch impart
Ideal figure, source of every art.
Time, motion, number, sunshine or the storm,
But mark varieties in Nature's form.

" Slow could the tangent organ[29] wander o'er
The rock-built mountain and the winding shore;
No apt ideas could the pigmy mite,
Or embryon emmet, to the touch excite.
But as each mass the solar ray reflects,
The eye's clear glass the transient beams collects;
Bends to their focal point the rays that swerve,
And paints the living image on the nerve.
So in some village-barn, or festive hall,
The spheric lens illumes the whiten'd wall;
O'er the bright field successive figures fleet,
And motley shadows dance along the sheet.
Symbol of solid forms is colour'd light,
And the mute language of the touch is sight.

" Hence in Life's portico starts young Surprise,
With step retreating and expanded eyes.
The virgin Novelty, whose radiant train
Soars o'er the clouds or sinks beneath the main,
With sweetly-mutable seductive charms
Thrills the young sense, the tender heart alarms.
Then Curiosity, with tracing hands
And meeting lips, the lines of form demands;

---

29 i.e. the hand [ed.]

Buoy'd on light step o'er ocean, earth, and sky,
Rolls the bright mirror of her restless eye;
While in wild groups tumultuous Passions stand,
And Lust and Hunger head the motley band;
Then Love and Rage succeed, and Hope and Fear;
And nameless vices close the gloomy rear;
Or young Philanthropy with voice divine
Convokes the adoring youth to Virtue's shrine;
Who with raised eye and pointing finger leads
To truths celestial and immortal deeds.

3 " As the pure language of the sight commands
The clear ideas furnish'd by the hands,
Beauty's fine forms attract our wondering eyes,
And soft alarms the pausing heart surprise.
Warm from its cell the tender infant born
Feels the cold chill of Life's aerial morn;
Seeks with spread hands the bosom's velvet orbs,
With closing lips the milky fount absorbs;
And, as compress'd the dulcet streams distil,
Drinks warmth and fragrance from the living rill;
Eyes with mute rapture every waving line;
Prints with adoring kiss the Paphian shrine,
And learns erelong, the perfect form confess'd,
Ideal Beauty from its mother's breast[30].

" Now on swift wheels descending, like a star,
Alights young Eros from his radiant car;
On angel-wings attendant Graces move,
And hail the God of Sentimental Love[31].
Earth at his feet extends her flowery bed,
And bends her silver blossoms round his head;
Dark clouds dissolve, the warring winds subside,
And smiling Ocean calms his tossing tide.
O'er the bright morn meridian lustres play,
And Heaven salutes him with a flood of day.

" Warm as the sun-beam, pure as driven snows,
The enamour'd god for young Dione glows;
Drops the still tear, with sweet attention sighs,
And woos the goddess with adoring eyes;

---

30 Our perception of beauty consists in our recognition by the sense of vision of those objects, first, which have before inspired our love...and, secondly, which bear any analogy of form to such objects.

31 'desire or sensation of beholding, embracing, and saluting a beautiful object' [*Zoonomia* XVI .6.1]

Marks her white neck beneath the gauze's fold,
Her ivory shoulders, and her locks of gold;
Drinks with mute ecstasy the transient glow
Which warms and tints her bosom's rising snow;
With holy kisses wanders o'er her charms,
And clasps the Beauty in Platonic arms;
Or, if the dewy hands of Sleep, unbid,
O'er her blue eyeballs close the lovely lid,
Watches each nascent smile and fleeting grace
That plays in day-dreams o'er her blushing face;
Counts the fine mazes of the curls, that break
Round her fair ear and shade her damask cheek;
Drinks the pure fragrance of her breath, and sips
With tenderest touch the roses of her lips;
O'er female hearts with chaste seduction reigns,
And binds society in silken chains.

4 " If the wide eye the wavy lawns explores,
The bending woodlands, or the winding shores;
Hills, whose green sides with soft protuberance rise,
Or the blue concave of the vaulted skies;
Or scans with nicer gaze the pearly swell
Of spiral volutes round the twisted shell;
Or undulating sweep, whose graceful turns
Bound the smooth surface of Etrurian urns.
When on fine forms the waving lines impress'd
Give the nice curves which swell the female breast,
The countless joys the tender Mother pours
Round the soft cradle of our infant hours
In lively trains of unextinct delight
Rise in our bosoms, recognized by sight.
Fond Fancy's eye recalls the form divine,
And Taste sits smiling upon Beauty's shrine.

" Where Egypt's pyramids gigantic stand,
And stretch their shadows o'er the shuddering sand,
Or where high rocks o'er ocean's dashing floods
Wave high in air their panoply of woods,
Admiring Taste delights to stray beneath
With eye uplifted, and forgets to breathe;
Or, as aloft his daring footsteps climb,
Crests their high summits with his arm sublime.

" Where mouldering columns mark the lingering wreck
Of Thebes, Palmyra, Babylon, Balbec,
The prostrate obelisk or shatter'd dome,
Uprooted pedestal and yawning tomb,

On loitering steps reflective Taste surveys
With folded arms and sympathetic gaze;
Charm'd with poetic Melancholy treads
O'er ruin'd towns and desolated meads;
Or rides sublime on Time's expanded wings,
And views the fate of ever-changing things.

" When Beauty's streaming eyes her woes express,
Or Virtue braves unmerited distress,
Love sighs in sympathy, with pain combined,
And new-born Pity charms the kindred mind;
The enamour'd Sorrow every cheek bedews,
And Taste, impassion'd, woos the tragic Muse.

" The rush-thatch'd cottage on the purple moor,
Where ruddy children frolic round the door;
The moss-grown antlers of the aged oak;
The shaggy locks that fringe the colt unbroke;
The bearded goat with nimble eyes, that glare
Through the long tissue of his hoary hair
(As with quick foot he climbs some ruin'd wall
And crops the ivy which prevents its fall);
With rural charms the tranquil mind delight,
And form a picture to the admiring sight;
While Taste with pleasure bends his eye, surprised
(In modern days) at Nature unchastised.

" The Genius-Form[32], on silver slippers borne,
With fairer dew-drops gems the rising morn;
Sheds o'er meridian skies a softer light,
And decks with brighter pearls the brow of night.
With finer blush the vernal blossom glows;
With sweeter breath enamour'd Zephyr blows;
The limpid streams with gentler murmurs pass,
And gayer colours tinge the watery glass;
Charm'd, round his steps along the enchanted groves
Flit the fine forms of Beauties, Graces, Loves.

5 " Alive, each moment of the transient hour,
When rest accumulates sensorial power,
The impatient senses, goaded to contract,
Forge new ideas, changing as they act;
And, in long streams dissever'd, or concrete
In countless tribes, the fleeting forms repeat,

[32] i.e. Taste [ed.]

Which rise excited in Volition's trains,
Or link the sparkling rings of Fancy's chains;
Or, as they flow from each translucent source,
Pursue Association's endless course.

" Hence when the inquiring hands with contact fine
Trace on hard forms the circumscribing line,
Which then the language of the rolling eyes
From distant scenes of earth and heaven supplies,
Those clear ideas of the touch and sight
Rouse the quick sense to anguish or delight.
Whence the fine power of Imitation springs,
And apes the outline of external things;
With ceaseless action to the world imparts
All moral virtues, languages and arts.
First the charm'd Mind mechanic powers collects:
Means for some end, and causes of effects;
Then learns from other minds their joys and fears,
Contagious smiles and sympathetic tears.

" What one fine stimulated sense discerns,
Another sense by Imitation learns.
So in the graceful dance, the step sublime
Learns from the ear the concordance of Time.
So, when the pen of some young artist prints
Recumbent nymphs in Titian's living tints,
The glowing limb, fair cheek, and flowing hair,
Respiring bosom, and seductive air,
He justly copies, with enamour'd sigh,
From Beauty's image pictured on his eye.

" Thus when great Angelo, in wondering Rome,
Fix'd the vast pillars of Saint Peter's dome,
Rear'd rocks on rocks sublime, and hung on high
A new Pantheon in the affrighted sky.
Each massy pier, now join'd and now aloof,
The figured architraves, and vaulted roof;
Aisles, whose broad curves gigantic ribs sustain,
Where holy echoes chant the adoring strain;
The central altar, sacred to the Lord,
Admired by sages, and by saints adored,
Whose brazen canopy ascends sublime
On spiral columns, unafraid of Time,
Were first by Fancy in ethereal dyes
Planed on the rolling tablets of his eyes;
And his true hand, with imitation fine,
Traced from his retina the grand design.

“ The Muse of Mimicry in every age
With silent language charms the attentive Stage:
The monarch’s stately step and tragic pause;
The hero bleeding in his country’s cause;
O’er her fond child the dying mother’s tears;
The lover’s ardour, and the virgin’s fears;
The tittering nymph that tries her comic task,
Bounds on the scene, and peeps behind her mask;
The Punch and Harlequin, and graver throng,
That shake the theatre with dance and song,
With endless trains of Angers, Loves, and Mirths,
Owe to the Muse of Mimicry their births.

“ Hence to clear images of form belong
The sculptor’s statue and the poet’s song,
The painter’s landscape and the builder’s plan;
And Imitation marks the mind of Man.

6 “ When strong desires or soft sensations move
The astonish’d intellect to rage or love,
Associate tribes of fibrous motions rise,
Flush the red cheek, or light the laughing eyes.
Whence ever-active Imitation finds
The ideal trains that pass in kindred minds;
Her mimic arts associate thoughts excite,
And the first language enters at the sight.

“ Thus jealous quails, or village cocks, inspect
Each other’s necks with stiffen’d plumes erect;
Smit with the wordless eloquence, they know
The rival passion of the threatening foe.
So when the famish’d wolves at midnight howl,
Fell serpents hiss, or fierce hyenas growl;
Indignant lions rear their bristling mail,
And lash their sides with undulating tail.
Or when the savage man with clenched fist
Parades, the scowling champion of the list,
With brandish’d arms, and eyes that roll to know
Where first to fix the meditated blow,
Association’s mystic power combines
Internal passions with external signs.

“ From these dumb gestures first the exchange began
Of viewless thought in bird, and beast, and Man;
And still the Stage, by mimic art, displays
Historic pantomime in modern days;

And hence the enthusiast orator affords
Force to the feebler eloquence of words.

" Thus the first language, when we frown'd or smiled,
Rose from the cradle, Imitation's child;
Next, to each thought associate sound accords,
And forms the dulcet symphony of words.
The tongue, the lips articulate; the throat
With soft vibration modulates the note:
Love, pity, war, the shout, the song, the prayer,
Form quick concussions of elastic air.

" Hence the first accents bear in airy rings
The vocal symbols of ideal things:
Name each nice change appulsive powers supply
To the quick sense of touch, or ear, or eye;
Or in fine traits abstracted forms suggest
Of Beauty, Wisdom, Number, Motion, Rest;
Or, as within reflex ideas[33] move,
Trace the light steps of Reason, Rage, or Love.
The next new sounds adjunctive[34] thoughts recite,
As hard, odorous, tuneful, sweet, or white.
The next the fleeting images select
Of action, suffering, causes, and effect;
Or mark existence with the march sublime
O'er earth and ocean of recording Time.

" The Giant Form on Nature's centre stands,
And waves in ether his unnumber'd hands;
Whirls the bright planets in their silver spheres,
And the vast Sun round other systems steers;
Till the last trump, amid the thunder's roar,
Sound the dread sentence, 'Time shall be no more!'

" Last steps Abbreviation, bold and strong,
And leads the volant trains of words along;
With sweet loquacity to Hermes springs,
And decks his forehead and his feet with wings.

7 " As the soft lips and pliant tongue are taught
With other minds to interchange the thought;
And sound, the symbol of the sense, explains
In parted links the long ideal trains;

---

33 the operations of our minds
34 concerning the properties of objects [ed.]

From clear conceptions of external things
The facile power of Recollection springs.

" Whence Reason's empire o'er the world presides,
And man from brute, and man from man, divides;
Compares and measures by imagined lines
Ellipses, circles, tangents, angles, sines;
Repeats with nice libration, and decrees
In what each differs, and in what agrees;
With quick volitions unfatigued selects
Means for some end, and causes of effects;
All human science worth the name imparts,
And builds on Nature's base the works of arts.

" The wasp, fine architect, surrounds his domes
With paper-foliage, and suspends his combs;
Secured from frost the bee industrious dwells,
And fills for winter all her waxen cells;
The cunning spider with adhesive line
Weaves his firm net immeasurably fine;
The wren, when embryon eggs her cares engross,
Seeks the soft down, and lines the cradling moss;
Conscious of change, the silkworm-nymphs begin
Attach'd to leaves their gluten threads to spin;
Then round and round they weave with circling heads
Sphere within sphere, and form their silken beds.
Say, did these fine volitions first commence
From clear ideas of the tangent sense,
From sires to sons by imitation caught,
Or in dumb language by tradition taught?
Or did they rise in some primeval site
Of larva-gnat, or microscopic mite,
And with instructive foresight still await
On each vicissitude of insect-state?
Wise to the present, nor to future blind,
They link the reasoning reptile to mankind!
Stoop, selfish Pride! survey thy kindred forms,
Thy brother-emmets, and thy sister-worms.

" Thy potent acts, Volition, still attend
The means of pleasure to secure the end;
To express his wishes and his wants design'd,
Language, the means, distinguishes Mankind;
For future works in Art's ingenious schools
His hands unwearied form and finish tools;
He toils for money future bliss to share,
And shouts to Heaven his mercenary prayer.

Sweet Hope delights him, frowning Fear alarms,
And Vice and Virtue court him to their arms.

" Unenvied eminence in Nature's plan
Rise the reflective faculties of Man!
Labour to Rest the thinking few prefer!
'Know but to mourn!' and 'Reason but to err!'
In Eden's groves, the cradle of the world,
Bloom'd a fair tree with mystic flowers unfurl'd;
On bending branches, as aloft it sprung,
Forbid to taste, the fruit of Knowledge hung;
Flow'd with sweet Innocence the tranquil hours,
And Love and Beauty warm'd the blissful bowers.
Till our deluded Parents pluck'd, erelong,
The tempting fruit, and gather'd Right and Wrong;
Whence Good and Evil, as in trains they pass,
Reflection imaged on her polish'd glass;
And Conscience felt, for blood by Hunger spilt,
The pains of shame, of sympathy, and guilt!

8 " Last, as observant Imitation stands,
Turns her quick glance and brandishes her hands,
With mimic acts associate thoughts excites,
And storms the soul with sorrows or delights,
Life's shadowy scenes are brighten'd and refined,
And soft emotions mark the feeling mind.

" The seraph Sympathy from Heaven descends,
And bright o'er Earth his beamy forehead bends:
On Man's cold heart celestial ardour flings,
And showers affection from his sparkling wings;
Rolls o'er the world his mild benignant eye,
Hears the lone murmur, drinks the whisper'd sigh;
Lifts the closed latch of pale Misfortune's door;
Opes the clench'd hand of Avarice to the poor;
Unbars the prison, liberates the slave;
Sheds his soft sorrows o'er the untimely grave;
Points with uplifted hand to realms above,
And charms the world with Universal Love.

" O'er the thrill'd frame his words assuasive steal,
And teach the selfish heart what others feel;
With sacred Truth each erring thought control,
Bind sex to sex, and mingle soul with soul.
'From Heaven,' he cries, 'descends the moral plan,
And gives Society to savage man.

High on yon scroll, inscribed o'er Nature's shrine,
Live in bright characters the words divine:
"In Life's disastrous scenes, to others do
What you would wish by others done to you."
Winds! wide o'er Earth the sacred law convey;
Ye Nations, hear it! and ye Kings, obey!'"

Unbreathing wonder hush'd the adoring throng,
Froze the broad eye, and chain'd the silent tongue.
Mute was the wail of Want, and Misery's cry,
And grateful Pity wiped her lucid eye.
Peace with sweet voice the seraph-form address'd,
And Virtue clasp'd him to her throbbing breast.

End of Canto Three

Canto Four

Of Good and Evil

" How few," the Muse in plaintive accents cries,
And mingles with her words pathetic sighs,
" How few, alas! in Nature's wide domains
The sacred charm of Sympathy restrains!
Uncheck'd desires from appetite commence,
And pure Reflection yields to selfish sense!
Blest is the sage who, learn'd in Nature's laws,
With nice distinction marks effect and cause;
Who views the insatiate grave with eye sedate,
Nor fears thy voice, inexorable Fate!

" When War, the demon, lifts his banner high,
And loud artillery rends the affrighted sky;
Swords clash with swords, on horses horses rush,
Man tramples man, and nations nations crush;
Death his vast scythe with sweep enormous wields,
And shuddering Pity quits the sanguine fields.

" The wolf, escorted by his milk-drawn dam,
Unknown to mercy, tears the guiltless lamb;
The towering eagle, darting from above,
Unfeeling rends the inoffensive dove;
The lamb and dove on living nature feed,
Crop the young herb, or crush the embryon seed.
Nor spares the loud owl in her dusky flight,
Smit with sweet notes, the minstrel of the night;
Nor spares, enamour'd of his radiant form,
The hungry nightingale the glowing worm,
Who with bright lamp alarms the midnight hour,
Climbs the green stem, and slays the sleeping flower.

" Fell oestrus[35] buries, in her rapid course,
Her countless brood in stag, or bull, or horse,
Whose hungry larva eats its living way,
Hatch'd by the warmth, and issues into day.
The wing'd ichneumon for her embryon young
Gores with sharp horn the caterpillar throng;
The cruel larva mines its silky course,
And tears the vitals of its fostering nurse.

---

35 gadfly

While fierce libellula[36] with jaws of steel
Ingulfs an insect-province at a meal.
Contending bee-swarms rise on rustling wings,
And slay their thousands with envenom'd stings.

" Yes! smiling Flora drives her armed car
Through the thick ranks of vegetable war:
Herb, shrub, and tree, with strong emotions rise
For light and air, and battle in the skies;
Whose roots diverging with opposing toil
Contend below for moisture and for soil.
Round the tall elm the flattering ivies bend,
And strangle, as they clasp, their struggling friend.
Envenom'd dews from Mancinella[37] flow,
And scald with caustic touch the tribes below.
Dense shadowy leaves on stems aspiring borne
With blight and mildew thin the realms of corn.
And insect hordes with restless tooth devour
The unfolded bud, and pierce the ravell'd flower.

" In ocean's pearly haunts, the waves beneath,
Sits the grim monarch of insatiate Death:
The shark rapacious, with descending blow,
Darts on the scaly brood that swims below.
The crawling crocodiles, beneath that move,
Arrest with rising jaw the tribes above.
With monstrous gape, sepulchral whales devour
Shoals at a gulp, a million in an hour.
Air, earth, and ocean, to astonish'd day
One scene of blood, one mighty tomb, display!
From Hunger's arms the shafts of Death are hurl'd,
And one great slaughter-house the warring world!

" The brow of Man erect, with thought elate,
Ducks to the mandate of resistless Fate;
Nor Love retains him, nor can Virtue save
Her sages, saints, or heroes from the grave.
While cold and hunger by defect oppress,
Repletion, heat, and labour by excess.
The whip, the sting, the spur, the fiery brand,
And, cursed Slavery! thy iron hand;

---

[36] dragonfly

[37] Hippomane: 'the dewdrops which fall from it are so caustic as to blister the skin, and produce dangerous ulcers, whence many have found their death by sleeping under its shade.' [ED's footnote to line 188 in 3.3]

And, led by Luxury, Disease's trains
Load human life with unextinguish'd pains.

" Here laughs Ebriety more fell than arms,
And thins the nations with her fatal charms;
With Gout and Hydrops groaning in her train,
And cold Debility, and grinning Pain;
With harlot-smiles deluded Man salutes,
Revenging all his cruelties to brutes!
There the curs'd spells of Superstition blind,
And fix her fetters on the tortured mind;
She bids in dreams tormenting shapes appear,
With shrieks that shock Imagination's ear;
E'en o'er the grave a deeper shadow flings,
And maddening Conscience darts a thousand stings.

" There writhing Mania sits on Reason's throne,
Or Melancholy marks it for her own,
Sheds o'er the scene a voluntary gloom,
Requests oblivion, and demands the tomb.
And last, Association's trains suggest
Ideal ills that harrow up the breast,
Call for the dead from Time's o'erwhelming main,
And bid departed Sorrow live again.

" Here ragged Avarice guards with bolted door
His useless treasures from the starving poor;
Loads the lorn hours with misery and care,
And lives a beggar to enrich his heir.
Unthinking crowds thy forms, Imposture, gull:
A saint in sackcloth, or a wolf in wool.
While mad with foolish fame, or drunk with power,
Ambition slays his thousands in an hour.
Demoniac Envy scowls with haggard mien
And blights the bloom of others' joys, unseen;
Or wrathful Jealousy invades the grove,
And turns to night meridian beams of Love!

" Here wide o'er earth impetuous waters sweep,
And fields and forests rush into the deep;
Or dread Volcano with explosion dire
Involves the mountains in a flood of fire;
Or yawning Earth, with closing jaws, inhumes
Unwarned nations, living in their tombs;
Or Famine seizes with her tiger-paw,
And swallows millions with unsated maw.

" There livid Pestilence, in league with Dearth,
Walks forth malignant o'er the shuddering Earth;
Her rapid shafts with airs volcanic wings,
Or steeps in putrid vaults her venom'd stings;
Arrests the young in beauty's vernal bloom,
And bears the innocuous strangers to the tomb!

" And now, e'en I, whose verse reluctant sings
The changeful state of sublunary things,
Bend o'er Mortality with silent sighs,
And wipe the secret tear-drops from my eyes;
Hear through the night one universal groan,
And mourn unseen for evils not my own;
With restless limbs and throbbing heart complain,
Stretch'd on the rack of sentimental pain!
Ah, where can Sympathy reflecting find
One bright idea to console the mind?
One ray of light in this terrene abode
To prove to Man the goodness of his God?"

2 " Hear, O ye Sons of Time!" the Nymph[38] replies,
Quick indignation darting from her eyes,
"When in soft tones the Muse lamenting sings,
And weighs with tremulous hand the sum of things,
She loads the scale in melancholy mood:
Presents the evil, but forgets the good.
But if the beam some firmer hand suspends,
And good and evil load the adverse ends,
With strong libration, where the good abides,
Quick nods the beam, the ponderous gold subsides.

" Hear, O ye Sons of Time! the powers of Life
Arrest the elements and stay their strife:
From wandering atoms, ethers, airs, and gas,
By combination form the organic mass;
And, as they seize, digest, secrete, dispense
The bliss of being to the vital ens.
Hence in bright groups from Irritation rise
Young Pleasure's trains, and roll their azure eyes.

" With fond delight we feel the potent charm
When Zephyrs cool us, or when sun-beams warm;
With fond delight inhale the fragrant flowers,
Taste the sweet fruits which bend the blushing bowers;

---

[38] i.e. Urania [ed.]

Admire the music of the vernal grove,
Or drink the raptures of delirious love.

" So with long gaze admiring eyes behold
The varied landscape all its lights unfold;
Huge rocks, opposing o'er the stream, project
Their naked bosoms, and the beams reflect;
Wave high in air their fringed crests of wood,
And chequer'd shadows dance upon the flood;
Green sloping lawns construct the sidelong scene
And guide the sparkling rill that winds between;
Conduct on murmuring wings the pausing gale,
And rural echoes talk along the vale.
Dim hills behind in pomp aerial rise,
Lift their blue tops, and melt into the skies.

" So when, by Handel tuned to measured sounds,
The trumpet vibrates or the drum rebounds,
Alarm'd we listen with ecstatic wonder
To mimic battles or imagined thunder.
When the soft lute in sweet impassion'd strains
Of cruel nymphs or broken vows complains,
As on the breeze the fine vibration floats,
We drink delighted the melodious notes.
But when young Beauty on the realms above
Bends her bright eye, and trills the tones of love,
Seraphic sounds enchant this nether sphere,
And listening angels lean from Heaven to hear.

" Next, by Sensation led, new joys commence
From the fine movements of the excited sense;
In swarms ideal urge their airy flight,
Adorn the day-scenes and illume the night.
Her spells o'er all the hand of Fancy flings,
Gives form and substance to unreal things,
With fruits and foliage decks the barren waste,
And brightens life with sentiment and taste.
Pleased, o'er the level and the rule presides,
The painter's brush, the sculptor's chisel guides;
With ray ethereal lights the poet's fire,
Tunes the rude pipe, or strings the heroic lyre.
Charm'd, round the Nymph on frolic footsteps move
The angelic forms of Beauty, Grace, and Love.

" So dreams the patriot, who indignant draws
The sword of vengeance in his Country's cause;

Bright for his brows unfading honours bloom,
Or kneeling virgins weep around his tomb.
So holy transports in the cloister's shade
Play round thy toilet, visionary Maid!
Charm'd o'er thy bed celestial voices sing,
And seraphs hover on enamour'd wing.

" So Howard, Moira, Burdett, sought the cells
Where want, or woe, or guilt in darkness dwells;
With Pity's torch illumed the dread domains,
Wiped the wet eye, and eased the galling chains;
With Hope's bright blushes warm'd the midnight air,
And drove from Earth the demon of Despair.
Erewhile emerging from the caves of night,
The friends of Man ascended into light;
With soft assuasive eloquence address'd
The ear of Power to stay his stern behest;
At Mercy's call to stretch his arm and save
His tottering victims from the gaping grave.
These with sweet smiles Imagination greets,
For these she opens all her treasured sweets,
Strews round their couch, by Pity's hand combined,
Bright flowers of joy, the sunshine of the mind;
While Fame's loud trump with sounds applausive breathes,
And Virtue crowns them with immortal wreaths.

" Thy acts, Volition, to the world impart
The plans of Science with the works of Art;
Give to proud Reason her comparing power,
Warm every clime, and brighten every hour.
In Life's first cradle ere the dawn began
Of young Society to polish Man,
The staff that propp'd him, and the bow that arm'd,
The boat that bore him, and the shed that warm'd;
Fire, raiment, food, the ploughshare, and the sword,
Arose, Volition, at thy plastic word.

" By thee instructed, Newton's eye sublime
Mark'd the bright periods of revolving time;
Explored in Nature's scenes the effect and cause,
And, charm'd, unravell'd all her latent laws.
Delighted Herschel with reflected light
Pursues his radiant journey through the night;
Detects new guards that roll their orbs afar
In lucid ringlets round the Georgian star.

" Inspired by thee, with scientific wand
Pleased Archimedes mark'd the figured sand;
Seized with mechanic grasp the approaching decks,
And shook the assailants from the inverted wrecks.
Then cried the Sage, with grand effects elate,
And proud to save the Syracusian state,
While crowds exulting shout their noisy mirth,
'Give where to stand, and I will move the Earth.'
So Savery guided his explosive steam
In iron cells to raise the balanced beam:
The Giant-form its ponderous mass uprears,
Descending nods, and seems to shake the spheres!

" Led by Volition on the banks of Nile
Where bloom'd the waving flax on Delta's isle,
Pleased Isis taught the fibrous stems to bind,
And part with hammers from the adhesive rind;
With locks of flax to deck the distaff-pole,
And whirl with graceful bend the dancing spool;
In level lines the length of woof to spread,
And dart the shuttle through the parting thread.
So Arkwright taught from cotton-pods to cull
And stretch in lines the vegetable wool;
With teeth of steel its fibre-knots unfurl'd,
And with the silver tissue clothed the world.

" Ages remote (by thee, Volition, taught)
Chain'd down in characters the winged thought;
With silent language mark'd the letter'd ground,
And gave to sight the evanescent sound.
Now, happier lot! enlighten'd realms possess
The learned labours of the immortal Press;
Nursed on whose lap the births of science thrive,
And rising Arts the wrecks of Time survive.

" Ye patriot heroes! in the glorious cause
Of Justice, Mercy, Liberty, and Laws,
Who call to Virtue's shrine the British youth,
And shake the senate with the voice of Truth,
Rouse the dull ear, the hoodwink'd eye unbind,
And give to energy the public mind.
While rival realms with blood unsated wage
Wide-wasting war with fell demoniac rage;
In every clime while army army meets,
And oceans groan beneath contending fleets,
Oh save, oh save, in this eventful hour
The tree of knowledge from the axe of Power;

With fostering peace the suffering nations bless,
And guard the freedom of the immortal Press!
So shall your deathless fame from age to age
Survive, recorded in the historic page;
And future bards with voice inspired prolong
Your sacred names, immortalized in song.

" Thy power, Association, next affords
Ideal trains annex'd to volant words;
Conveys to listening ears the thought superb,
And gives to Language her expressive verb;
Which in one changeful sound suggests the fact
At once to be, to suffer, or to act,
And marks on rapid wing o'er every clime
The viewless flight of evanescent Time.

" Call'd by thy voice, contiguous thoughts embrace
In endless streams, arranged by time or place.
The Muse historic[39] hence in every age
Gives to the world her interesting page;
While in bright landscape, from her moving pen,
Rise the fine tints of manners and of men.

" Call'd by thy voice, Resemblance next describes
Her sister-thoughts in lucid trains or tribes;
Whence pleased Reflection oft combines
By loose analogies her fair designs;
Each winning grace of polish'd wit bestows
To deck the Nymphs of Poetry and Prose.

" Last, at thy potent nod, Effect and Cause
Walk hand in hand, accordant to thy laws;
Rise at Volition's call, in groups combined,
Amuse, delight, instruct, and serve Mankind;
Bid raised in air the ponderous structure stand,
Or pour obedient rivers through the land;
With cars unnumber'd crowd the living streets,
Or people oceans with triumphant fleets.

" Thy magic touch imagined forms supplies
From colour'd light, the language of the eyes;
On Memory's page departed hours inscribes:
Sweet scenes of youth, and Pleasure's vanish'd tribes.

[39] Clio, Urania's sister-muse [ed.]

By thee Antinous leads the dance sublime
On wavy step, and moves in measured time;
Charm'd, round the youth successive Graces throng,
And Ease conducts him as he moves along;
Unbreathing crowds the floating form admire,
And vestal bosoms feel forbidden fire.

" When rapt Cecilia breathes her matin vow,
And lifts to Heaven her fair adoring brow,
From her sweet lips and rising bosom part
Impassion'd notes that thrill the melting heart;
Tuned by thy hand the dulcet harp she rings,
And sounds responsive echo from the strings;
Bright scenes of bliss in trains suggested move,
And charm the world with melody and love.

3 " Soon the fair forms with vital being bless'd,
Time's feeble children, lose the boon possess'd;
The goaded fibre ceases to obey,
And sense deserts the uncontractile clay;
While births unnumber'd, ere the parents die,
The hourly waste of lovely life supply;
And thus, alternating with death, fulfil
The silent mandates of the Almighty Will,
Whose hand unseen the works of Nature dooms
By laws unknown: who gives, and who resumes[40].

" Each pregnant oak ten thousand acorns forms,
Profusely scatter'd by autumnal storms;
Ten thousand seeds each pregnant poppy sheds,
Profusely scatter'd from its waving heads;
The countless aphides, prolific tribe,
With greedy trunks the honey'd sap imbibe,
Swarm on each leaf with eggs or embryons big,
And pendent nations tenant every twig.
Amorous with double sex, the snail and worm
Scoop'd in the soil their cradling caverns form;
Heap their white eggs secure from frost and floods,
And crowd their nurseries with uncounted broods.
Ere yet with wavy tail the tadpole swims,
Breathes with new lungs or tries his nascent limbs,
Her countless shoals the amphibious frog forsakes,
And living islands float upon the lakes.

[40] takes back, gives again [JD]

The migrant herring steers her myriad bands
From seas of ice to visit warmer strands;
Unfathom'd depths and climes unknown explores,
And covers with her spawn unmeasured shores.
All these, increasing by successive birth,
Would each o'erpeople ocean, air, and earth.

" So human progenies, if unrestrain'd,
By climate friended and by food sustain'd,
O'er seas and soils prolific hordes would spread
Erelong, and deluge their terraqueous bed.
But war and pestilence, disease and dearth,
Sweep the superfluous myriads from the earth.
The while[41] new forms reviving tribes acquire
Each passing moment, as the old expire
(Like insects swarming in the noontide bower
Rise into being, and exist an hour).
The births and deaths contend with equal strife,
And every pore of Nature teems with life,
Which buds or breathes from Indus to the Poles,
And Earth's vast surface kindles, as it rolls!

" Hence when a monarch or a mushroom dies,
Awhile extinct the organic matter lies;
But, as a few short hours or years revolve,
Alchemic powers the changing mass dissolve.
Born to new life unnumber'd insects pant;
New buds surround the microscopic plant,
Whose embryon senses and unwearied frames
Feel finer goads and blush with purer flames.
Renascent Joys from Irritation spring,
Stretch the long root, or wave the aurelian wing.

" When thus a squadron or an army yields,
And festering carnage loads the waves or fields;
When few from famines or from plagues survive,
Or earthquakes swallow half a realm alive;
While Nature sinks in Time's destructive storms,
The wrecks of Death are but a change of forms.
Emerging Matter from the grave returns,
Feels new desires, with new sensations burns;
With youth's first bloom a finer sense acquires,
And Loves and Pleasures fan the rising fires.

[41] i.e. 'meanwhile'. 'The while' is D. King-Hele's emendation of the original 'Thus while'. [ed.]

Thus sainted Paul 'O Death!' exulting cries,
'Where is thy sting? O Grave! thy victories?'

" Immortal Happiness from realms deceased
Wakes as from sleep, unlessen'd or increased;
Calls to the wise in accents loud and clear;
Soothes with sweet tones the sympathetic ear;
Informs and fires the revivescent clay,
And lights the dawn of Life's returning day.

" So when Arabia's Bird, by age oppress'd,
Consumes delighted on his spicy nest,
A filial Phoenix from his ashes springs,
Crowned with a star, on renovated wings;
Ascends exulting from his funeral flame
And soars and shines, another and the same.

" So erst the Sage[42], with scientific truth,
In Grecian temples taught the attentive youth
With ceaseless change how restless atoms pass
From life to life, a transmigrating mass.
How the same organs which today compose
The poisonous henbane, or the fragrant rose,
May with tomorrow's sun new forms compile:
Frown in the Hero, in the Beauty smile.
Whence drew the enlighten'd Sage the moral plan
That man should ever be the friend of man;
Should eye with tenderness all living forms,
His brother-emmets, and his sister-worms.

" Hear, O ye Sons of Time! your final doom,
And read the characters that mark your tomb:
The marble mountain and the sparry steep
Were built by myriad nations of the deep,
Age after age, who form'd their spiral shells,
Their sea-fan gardens and their coral cells,
Till central fires, with unextinguish'd sway,
Raised the primeval islands into day.
The sand-fill'd strata stretch'd from Pole to Pole,
Unmeasured beds of clay, and marl, and coal;
Black ore of manganese, the zinky stone,
And dusky steel on his magnetic throne,
In deep morass, or eminence superb,
Rose from the wrecks of animal or herb.

---

[42] Pythagoras [ed.]

These from their elements by life combined,
Form'd by digestion, and in glands refined,
Gave, by their just excitement of the sense,
The bliss of being to the vital ens.

" Thus the tall mountains that emboss the lands,
Huge isles of rock, and continents of sands,
Whose dim extent eludes the inquiring sight,
ARE MIGHTY MONUMENTS OF PAST DELIGHT.
Shout round the globe how Reproduction strives
With vanquish'd Death, and Happiness survives;
How Life increasing peoples every clime,
And young renascent Nature conquers Time;
And high in golden characters record
The immense munificence of Nature's Lord!

" He gives and guides the Sun's attractive force,
And steers the planets in their silver course;
With heat and light revives the golden day,
And breathes his spirit on organic clay;
With hand unseen directs the General Cause
By firm immutable immortal laws."

Charm'd with her words, the Muse astonish'd stands;
The Nymphs enraptured clasp their velvet hands;
Applausive thunder from the fane recoils,
And holy echoes peal along the aisles;
O'er Nature's shrine celestial lustres glow,
And lambent glories circle round her brow.

4 Now sinks the golden sun; the vesper song
Demands the tribute of Urania's tongue.
Onward she steps, her fair associates calls
From leaf-wove avenues and vaulted halls.
Fair virgin trains in bright procession move,
Trail their long robes, and whiten all the grove;
Pair after pair to Nature's Temple sweep,
Thread the broad arch, ascend the winding steep.
Through brazen gates, along susurrant aisles,
Stream round their Goddess the successive files;
Curve above curve to golden seats retire,
And star with beauty the refulgent quire.

And first to Heaven the consecrated throng
With chant alternate pour the adoring song;
Swell the full hymn, now high, and now profound,
With sweet responsive symphony of sound.

Seen through their wiry harps, below, above,
Nods the fair brow, the twinkling fingers move;
Soft-warbling flutes the ruby lip commands,
And cymbals ring with high uplifted hands.

To Chaos next the notes melodious pass:
How suns exploded from the kindling mass,
Waved o'er the vast inane their tresses bright,
And charm'd young Nature's opening eyes with light.
Next from each sun how spheres reluctant burst,
And second planets issued from the first.
And then to Earth descends the moral strain:
How isles, emerging from the shoreless main,
With sparkling streams and fruitful groves began,
And form'd a paradise for mortal man.

Sublimer notes record Celestial Love,
And high rewards in brighter climes above;
How Virtue's beams with mental charm engage
Youth's raptured eye and warm the frost of age;
Gild with soft lustre Death's tremendous gloom,
And light the dreary chambers of the tomb.
How fell Remorse shall strike with venom'd dart,
Though mail'd in adamant, the guilty heart;
Fierce Furies drag to pains and realms unknown
The blood-stain'd tyrant from his tottering throne.

By hands unseen are struck aerial wires,
And angel-tongues are heard amid the quires.
From aisle to aisle the trembling concord floats,
And the wide roof returns the mingled notes.
Through each fine nerve the keen vibrations dart,
Pierce the charm'd ear and thrill the echoing heart.

Mute the sweet voice and still the quivering strings,
Now Silence hovers on unmoving wings.
Slow to the altar fair Urania bends
Her graceful march, the sacred steps ascends;
High in the midst with blazing censer stands,
And scatters incense with illumined hands;
Thrice to the Goddess bows with solemn pause,
With trembling awe the mystic veil withdraws,
And, meekly kneeling on the gorgeous shrine,
Lifts her ecstatic eyes to Truth Divine!

The End

A GLOSSARY (1) of Historical Personages Appearing in the Poem

Antony, Saint, of Padua (1195-1231), Franciscan friar and reputed miracle worker
Archimedes (287 – 212BC), natural philosopher
Arkwright, Sir Richard (1732-92), textile industrialist and inventor
Bacon, Roger (c.1219-92), Franciscan friar, proto-scientist
Beccari, Jacopo Bartolommeo (1682-1766), Italian alchemist\chemist
Boyle, Robert (1627-91), chemist and physicist
Brindley, James (1716-72), pioneer canal builder
Burdett, Sir Francis (1770-1844), radical reformer
Cecilia, Roman saint and martyr of the third century, patron saint of music
Crewe, Miss Emma, painter and original illustrator of *The Botanic Garden*
Damer, Hon. Mrs Anne Seymour (1748-1828), sculptor
Day, John (d.1774), pioneer diving-bell submariner
Delany, Mrs Mary (1700-88), creator of series of paper-mosaic flowers
Devon: William Cavendish, Fifth Duke of Devonshire (1748 – 1811)
Emma, (Queen) (d.1052), said to have undergone ordeal by fire
Foster, Lady Elizabeth, second wife of the Fifth Duke of Devonshire
Franklin, Benjamin (1706-90), printer, scientist, statesman
Fuseli, J.H. (1741 – 1825), Swiss-born painter based in London
George III (1738-1820), King from 1760 till 1820
Handel, George Frederick (1685-1759), composer
Herschel, Sir William Frederick (1738-1822), astronomer, discovered Uranus in 1781
Howard, John (1726-90), prison reformer
Jones: 'A young lady who devotes a great part of an ample fortune to well chosen acts of secret charity.' [ED]
Kirwan, Richard (1733-1812), chemist, geologist, climatologist
Kun[c]kel, Johann (1630/8-1703), Prussian chemist
Linnaeus, Carolus (1707-78), pioneer taxonomer, botanist – the "Swedish sage"
Melbourn, Lady Elizabeth Melbourne, political hostess. Her son, Lord M. (b.1779) later became Prime Minister.
Michelangelo Buonarroti (1475 – 1564), Renaissance sculptor, painter, architect, poet
Michell, John (1724-93), Cambridge mathematician and physicist
Milcena: Mrs Millicent French (1745/6-89), highly skilled 'in botany and natural history' [ED]
Moira: Francis Rawdon, Second Earl of Moira (1754-1826), political reformer
Molesworth, Lady, reported in *The Gentleman's Magazine*, Vol. XXXIII [1763] as losing her life together with the lives of two of her five daughters on the 6th May of that year in a house fire
Montgolfier, Joseph Michel (1740-1810), pioneer balloonist
Mundy, F.N.C. (1739-1815), poet, author of *Needwood Forest*
Newton, Sir Isaac (1642-1727), Cambridge mathematician and physicist
Ninon: Ninon de Lenclos (1620-1705), 'a Frenchwoman noted for her beauty and wit' [Oxford Companion to Literature]
Pierce, Captain, went down with Haslewell East-Indiaman, 1786
Priestley, Joseph (1733-1804), clergyman, political radical, pioneer chemist
Pythagoras (c530-500BC), Greek mathematician and philosopher

Richman, Georg Wilhelm (1711-53), Professor of Natural Philosophy, St Petersburg
Rosiere: Pilatre de Rosier, J.F. (1756-85), made first ever balloon flight, Paris 1783; died in balloon accident
Roubiliac, Louis-Francois (c.1695-1762), late- Baroque sculptor based in London
Savery, Thomas (1650-1715), engineer and inventor
Shakespeare, William (1564-1616), poet and dramatist
Spalding, Mr, pioneer diving-bell submariner, died underwater in 1783
Titian (1488/90-1576), Renaissance painter of the School of Venice
Torricelli, Evangelista (1608-47), Italian physicist, discoverer of air pressure
Wedgwood, Josiah (1730-95), pioneer pottery manufacturer and industrialist
Woodmason: family suffering household fire
Wright [of Derby], Joseph (1734-97), painter

A GLOSSARY (2) of Classical References Appearing in the Poem

Achelous	most important of the Greek river gods
Adonis	vegetation god, loved by Aphrodite (Venus)
Aeneas	Trojan hero, son of Anchises and Aphrodite
Aeson	father of Jason; restored to youth by Medea
Ant[a]eus	giant son of Poseidon and Gaia, strangled by Hercules
Antinous	chief among the suitors of Penelope, wife of Odysseus
Anubis	Egyptian dog-headed god of the dead
Apollo	powerful, handsome, youthful god of the arts; as Phoebus Apollo he is a sun god
Aquarius	constellation of the Water-bearer
Arachne	Lydian princess who challenged Athena in weaving and was jealously transformed by the goddess into a spider
Argo	southern constellation; the ship in which Jason sailed to Colchis in search of the golden fleece
Argos	one of the earliest settled regions in the Peloponnese
Atrides	joint designation of Agamemnon and Menelaus, sons of Atreus
Auster	south wind
Bellona	Roman goddess of war
Boreas	north wind
Cacus	in Roman myth the giant son of Vulcan; he was killed in his cave by Hercules in retaliation for losing half the cattle of Geryon to him through theft
Caduceus	the wand of the messenger god Hermes
Cambyses	king of the Medes and Persians
Cassiopeia	constellation; Cassiopeia was the mother of Andromeda
Cepheus	constellation; Cepheus was the father of Andromeda
Ceres	Roman goddess of agriculture and of edible plants; equivalent to the Greek goddess Demeter
Cestus	girdle worn by Venus which attracted love to the wearer

Chaos	Greek concept of the void that existed before the creation of the cosmos
Charybdis	Homeric sea-monster that sucked in and spewed out water; a whirlpool in the sea between Sicily and Italy
Clotho	as one of the three Fates, she spun the thread of life
Colchis	country by the Black Sea and legendary home of Medea; the Argonauts sailed there in search of the golden fleece
Creusa (1)	also known as Glauke, daughter of King Creon of Corinth; Jason desired her as his second wife to replace Medea
Creusa (2)	daughter of Priam and Hecuba; wife to Aeneas
Cupid	Roman god of love, represented as child-like with bow and arrows; son of Venus
Cyclops	three giant sons of Uranus and Gaia, with a single central eye
Cynthia	goddess of the moon; synonymous with Artemis in Greek myth and with the Roman goddess Diana
Cyprian Queen	Venus, who at her birth rose fully formed from the sea near Cyprus
Daedalus	ingenious metal artificer in Athens; father of Icarus
Dejanira	wife of Hercules
Diana	Roman virgin-goddess of the moon and of hunting
Dione	wife of Jupiter, mother of Venus; name sometimes used of Venus herself, as here by Darwin
Dis	Pluto, god of the underworld
Draco	constellation; a dragon or snake in Greek and Roman myth
Dryad	nymph of woods and forests
Echo	Greek nymph, daughter of Gaia; confidante of Zeus, whose wife, Hera, deprived her of the power of independent speech
Eleusis	Greek city northwest of Athens, centre of cult of Demeter celebrating the return of Persephone from the underworld; initiates looked for happiness in the afterlife
Elysium	the Greek land of the blest at the western edge of the world
Eolus [Aeolus]	the god of all the winds
Eros	Greek god of love, associated in Hesiod with the origin of the cosmos; in Roman mythology he becomes Cupid, the playful winged archer promoting amorous liaisons
Europa	princess of Tyre; carried into Crete by Jupiter in the form of a white bull
Eurus	east wind
Favonius	west wind and as such the herald of spring
Fawn [Faun]	Roman god of the countryside, lustful in nature
Flora	Roman goddess of flowers and gardens; she occasionally assumes some attributes of a goddess of love
Furies	triple Roman goddesses of revenge
Galatea	a nereid; her name in Greek means 'she who is milk white'
Gorgon	winged monster with snakes for hair, who could turn victims to stone with a glance. One of the three Gorgons was Medusa

Graces	the Roman goddesses Aglaia, Thalia, and Euphrosyne; attendants on Venus and the Muses
Griffin	fabulous creature with the winged body of a lion and the head of an eagle
Harpy	gigantic bird with a human female head; in habit a 'snatcher'
Hebe	Greek goddess of youthful beauty; a wife of Herakles
Helen	Homeric heroine, noted for her beauty; her abduction by Paris to Troy triggered the Trojan war
Helicon	mountain-range in Boeotia, the seat of the Muses
Hercules	Latin equivalent of the Greek Herakles; he was born with great strength and performed the following twelve labours: i) killed the Nemean lion ii) overcame the Hydra iii) captured the golden-horned Arcadian stag iv) captured the Erymanthian boar v) cleaned the Augean stables vi) destroyed the man-eating Stymphalian birds vii) captured the Cretan bull viii) tamed the man-eating Thracian mares ix) obtained the girdle of the Amazon–queen, Hippolyta x) stole the cattle belonging to the monster, Geryon xi) obtained the golden apples of the Hesperides xii) brought Cerberus, the triple-headed watchdog, out of the underworld
Hermes	messenger of the Greek gods; equivalent to the Roman god Mercury
Hero	priestess of Venus, loved by Leander
Hesper[us]	the evening star; also known as Vesper
Hybla	mountain in Sicily, known for its bees and wild thyme
Hydra	nine-headed serpent monster of Lake Lerna in Greek mythology
Hygeia	Greek goddess of health
Hymen	Greek god of marriage
Icarus	son of Daedalus; he flew on his father's waxen wings too close to the sun and plunged to his death in the sea
Idalian	byname of Venus, taken from Idalion in Cyprus, a place sacred to Aphrodite (Venus)
Ida [Ide]	mountain near Troy; location of many Greek legends
Iris	golden-winged messenger of Zeus and Hera; personification of the rainbow
Isis	Egyptian mother-goddess; wife of Osiris
Jason	Greek hero who, with the Argonauts, sailed to fetch the Golden Fleece from Colchis; son of Aeson and Alkimeda; husband of Medea
Jove [Jupiter]	king of the gods; equivalent to the Greek god Zeus
Jove's bird	the eagle

Juno	queen of the Roman gods and wife of Jupiter
Laocoon	high priest of Apollo, killed with his two sons by sea-serpents
Leander	the lover of Hero; he often swam the Hellespont to visit her
Leda	daughter of King Thestius of Aetolia; made love to by Zeus in the form of a swan; mother of Helen
Lerna	lake home of the Hydra
Lethe	river of oblivion in the Greek underworld of Hades
Mars	Roman god of war and lover of Venus
Medea	sorceress who helped Jason to acquire the golden fleece
Medusa	one of the three Gorgons: monsters who could turn victims to stone
Memnon	king of Ethiopia who fought for the Trojans; a statue at Thebes was thought by the Greeks to be of Memnon and to produce a musical sound at dawn
Memphis	celebrated city of Egypt
Minerva	Roman goddess of artisans, poets, teachers and physicians; equivalent to the Greek goddess Athena, goddess of power and wisdom
Muses	mistresses of the sciences and the arts; governors of the feasts of the gods; companions of the Graces and of Apollo
Naiad	river-nymph
Narcissus	Greek youth who rejected the nymph Echo and was punished by being changed into a flower
Nemea	forest home of the lion killed by Herakles
Nereid	sea-nymph
Niobe	in Greek legend, the daughter of Tantalus and Dione. Her fourteen children were killed by Diana, and she became a weeping statue in her grief
Olympia	deified sanctuary of Zeus in the western Peloponnese
Olympus	mountain home of the gods in northern Greece
Orpheus	musician-god whose lyre had the power to charm men and gods; he led his wife Eurydice out of Hades. He was later dismembered by the women of Thrace
Pan	Greek god of flocks and herds, player of the Syrinx [pipes]; equivalent to the Roman god Sylvanus
Paphian groves	groves sacred to Venus
Paris	son of King Priam of Troy, abductor of Helen, initiator of the Trojan war
Philomel[a]	in Latin literature, a nymph pursued by Tereus and changed into a nightingale
Phoenix	mythical bird resurrected from its own ashes, symbolising immortality for the Greeks
Plenty's horn	cornucopia: the horn of the river-god Achelous filled with fruit and flowers
Pluto	Greek god of the earth's treasures and lord of the underworld
Pomona	Roman goddess of gardens and fruit trees

Prometheus	Greek Titan who brought culture and fire to mankind, for which he was punished by Zeus, being chained by Vulcan to a rock in the Caucasus while a vulture (or eagle) daily fed on his liver
Proserpina	goddess of the underworld and of the regenerative cycle of vegetation; daughter of Ceres; venerated in the Eleusinian Mysteries. Roman equivalent to the Greek Persephone
Proteus	Greek sea-god who possessed the gifts of self-transformation and of prophecy
Psyche	Greek goddess of pleasure, loved by Cupid
Pythian Laura	Pythonissa, oracular priestess of Apollo
Saturnia	daughter of Saturn; equivalent to Juno
Saturn	Roman god of agriculture
Satyr	lustful, drunken, woodland god
Scamander	river near Troy
Scylla	sea monster living under dangerous rocks in the straits of Messina
Selene	Greek goddess of the moon, equivalent to the Roman Diana
Sirens	fabulous creatures with the bodies of birds and the heads of women; they embody the allure of sensuality
Tantalus	son of Zeus, father of Niobe. Divulged secrets to humanity and was tormented by having food and drink in view but withheld
Thalestris	Amazon queen
Thyrsus	the wand of Dionysus
Triton	sea-god with human body and tail of a fish
Trophonius	oracle in caves at Lebadea in Boeotia, only consulted at night; suppliants characteristically returned in deep melancholy
Urania	muse of astronomy whose attributes are the globe and compass. Also a byname for Aphrodite
Venus	Roman goddess of love; equivalent to the Greek Aphrodite
Vestal	virgin priestess of Vesta, the Roman goddess and guardian of the sacred flame of hearth and home
Vulcan	Roman smith-god of fire, husband of Venus; equivalent to the Greek god of forge, fire, and of artisans, Hephaestos, lame son of Zeus and Hera
Zephyr	west wind; equivalent to Favonius. Often used, as by Darwin, for any light wind